ARE WE HAVING FUN YET?

ARE WE HAVING

FUN YET?

ENJOYING THE OUTDOORS WITH PARTNERS, FAMILIES, AND GROUPS

BRIAN BAIRD, PH.D.

ILLUSTRATIONS BY DAVID HORSEY

THE
MOUNTAINEERS

Published by
The Mountaineers
1001 SW Klickitat Way, Suite 201
Seattle, Washington 98134

© 1995 by Brian Baird

9 8 7 6 5
5 4 3 2 1

No part of this book may be reproduced in any form, or by any electronic, mechanical, or other means, without permission in writing from the publisher.

Published simultaneously in Canada by Douglas & McIntyre, Ltd., 1615 Venables Street, Vancouver, B.C. V5L 2H1

Published simultaneously in Great Britain by Cordee, 3a DeMontfort Street, Leicester, England, LE1 7HD

Manufactured in the United States of America

Edited by Kris Fulsaas
Cover design by Watson Graphics
Illustrations by David Horsey
Book design and typography by The Mountaineers Books

Cover photographs: *Left:* Stream-crossing hikers © Joel W. Rogers/Tony Stone Images. *Right:* Children with parents getting ready for camping trip © Arthur Tilley/Tony Stone Images.

Library of Congress Cataloging-in-Publication Data
Baird, Brian.
    Are we having fun yet? : enjoying the outdoors with partners, families, and
    groups / Brian Baird.
        p.   cm.
    Includes index.
    ISBN 0-89886-449-6
    1. Outdoor recreation—United States—Handbooks, manuals, etc.
    2. Family recreation—United States—Handbooks, manuals, etc.   I. Title.
    GV191.4.B336   1995
    796.5'0973—dc20   95–550
                                                                  CIP

CONTENTS

To my wife Mary, to my family, and to everyone who works to protect the natural environment

PREFACE

SOMEWHERE, VERY NEAR, A GRAY WHALE WAS BREATHING. We were camped on the dunes of Magdalena Bay, and a just-past-full moon was beginning to rise. We slipped our kayaks into the dark waters and gently paddled toward the sound. The whale breathed again. Closer now, we stopped paddling and brought the kayaks together. As we waited in the darkness, I listened to my own breath, and the pounding of my heart. We knew we were close, but how close?

We stared into the night and listened. Then we were confused. Directly in front of us a light appeared in the water, then another light beside the first. At last the awareness came. Two whales, a mother and a newborn, had surfaced before us and the moon was reflecting off their backs. They breathed again, sending a fountain of steam into the moonlight. The mist drifted over us and small droplets touched our faces.

I do not know how long we were there. We sat motionless, holding hands across our kayaks and saying nothing, drifting together as the moon rose higher. Every few minutes the whales sent mist that glistened like stars into the night. Then, with no sound, they were gone.

If we are lucky, life sometimes gives us moments that are sublime. If we are very lucky, we can share those moments with others and they are never lost. In those instants, whatever troubles may have come before, and whatever may come after, seem far removed.

This book is written to help people make the most of their time together outdoors. My hope is that it will make for fewer hard times and more good times. As you work on your own and with your partners to improve relationships, keep in mind that anything worth learning takes time and practice. You are bound to make mistakes, and it would be unrealistic to expect everything to be perfect the minute you finish reading this book.

Just as part of the fun of outdoor activities comes from watching ourselves and our partners make progress, the same is true of outdoor relationships. When preparation together prevents problems from developing, when situations that might have once provoked a conflict are handled cooperatively, when partners work constructively together to make sure everyone has fun, you'll know you're making progress.

Throughout this book I have included stories of events that people shared from their own relationships as well as incidents drawn from personal experiences. I have included these in the hope that readers can learn from the successes and mistakes of others. Out of respect for the privacy of those whose stories are reported here, I have used different names and in some instances have made minor changes in certain details. Thus, if there are any similarities to actual persons or events, this is coincidental.

ACKNOWLEDGMENTS

THIS BOOK REFLECTS YEARS OF PERSONAL EXPERIENCES with family and friends as well as the input of hundreds of people who were kind enough to offer their input through interviews and surveys. To everyone who contributed and with whom I have shared the outdoors, I am deeply grateful.

I also want to take this opportunity to express my appreciation to those whose input has been of special importance. During many happy years camping and hiking in the mountains and canyons of Colorado, my parents, William and Edith Baird, taught me the joy of the outdoors and the importance of believing in possibilities. My brother Bruce and sister Maggie continue to give support and to remind me of the gift of family. On countless backpacking and climbing trips, my good friends Steve Richardson and Russ Williams have marveled with me at the Colorado night sky. I remember the alpenglow sunsets shared in the Cascades and Olympics with John Schubert, Ivar Schuholm, Robert Liberty, Perry and Lynn Rose, Bob Permann, and others. I hope we'll continue to be amazed together for years to come. For introducing me to white-water kayaking, I owe thanks to Mark Kiefner, and to Steve Daley, who later brought me along and was a wonderful teacher. On and off the water, Tim Jacobsen continues to be a good friend. From the Grand Canyon to Idaho and the rivers of Europe, I will always cherish the spirit and kindness of Gert and Marlis; Gerd, Vera, and Mariana; Thomas and Ulli; and the members of the BKV. For teaching me so many things about people and about myself, I will forever be indebted to my friend and colleague Rita Valentine and to Sharon Rue. Others to thank include my running partner Kirk Isakson, my friends from Asturias, and the many students who have given me the privilege of traveling and learning with them. I also want to thank The Mountaineers Books, and especially Donna DeShazo, Cynthia Newman Bohn, Linda Gunnarson, and Kris Fulsaas. Their many valuable suggestions made this book possible and improved it in countless ways. Finally, I am profoundly grateful for the love, friendship, and encouragement of my wife, Mary Baird.

AN INVITATION

I hope this book is helpful and that you will share it with others you know who love the outdoors. I also want to invite you to send me any suggestions you have for how the book could be improved in future editions. I am always open to new ideas and I'm sure each reader will discover things that could help others in their relationships. If you have suggestions or stories you want to share, please write me at the address below.

—Brian Baird
Department of Psychology
Pacific Lutheran University
Tacoma, WA 98447

INTRODUCTION

"Why is it that when I'm doing my favorite thing in the world with my favorite person in the world, things never seem to work right?"

"If we're not having fun, something needs to change."

CHOOSE ANY OUTDOOR ACTIVITY and you are sure to find dozens of books telling you what equipment you need, how to improve your skills, and the best places to go. This book is different. This is about the greatest outdoor challenge of all—getting along with each other and with ourselves.

Ideally, being together outdoors should make relationships stronger and outdoor experiences more fun. Sometimes that happens, but it also happens that things don't go as well as we would hope. Either a relationship makes it harder to enjoy the outdoors or the outdoors makes it harder to enjoy a relationship.

The goal of this book is to help you and your partners, family, and friends make the most of being outdoors together. As with every activity, it takes time and effort to develop your skills, but the more skill you have the more fun you can have. In thiscase, the skills do not involve technical expertise or physical ability. Rather, they include understanding and communicating with one another and dealing effectively with stressful situations together. Developing these skills is worth the effort because they apply to all our outdoor activities and to the rest of our lives. Each time you go into the outdoors you have an opportunity to learn more about yourself and relationships.

VOICES FROM THE WILDERNESS

One of my goals in writing this book was to gather information from as many people as possible. Whenever I met couples, friends, families, or groups involved in the outdoors, I asked if they would mind being interviewed for the book. In the interviews, we discussed what works for people in their outdoor relationships, what doesn't work, great relationship success stories, and how "relationship accidents" happened. For the better part of three years, a notepad was always at the ready. I spoke with people from throughout the United States and Canada as well as friends and fellow travelers from many other countries. I interviewed backpackers on the trail, skiers on chair lifts, kayakers, canoeists, climbers, cyclists, and others wherever I found them. Many whom I could not meet with directly were kind enough to send their ideas by mail through surveys and letters. I also spoke with organized outings groups and leaders as well as professional outdoor guides and instructors. Almost everyone I approached seemed eager to share stories and offer suggestions. The input of all those people is reflected throughout this book.

In addition to the ideas of others, I have also drawn upon my own experiences. From the time I was a child in Colorado, skiing, backpacking, and later on kayaking and climbing virtually defined who I was. Along the way I have been a ski instructor, have led groups of students on hiking and kayaking trips, and have been part of countless trips with friends and family. Now, with a family of my own, those activities continue to be a central element of what I do and who I am. Not surprisingly, this background has given me plenty of stories to draw upon for this book.

The other part of my identity, which is also reflected in this book, is my training and practice as a clinical psychologist. After almost twenty years of practice with individuals, couples, and families, I like to think I've learned a few things that can help folks get along a little better. In this book I have tried to keep the "psycho-babble" to a minimum, but I have included selected ideas from psychology that are useful to outdoor relationships.

TURNING FEARS INTO OPPORTUNITIES FOR FUN

One of the things I discovered from my interviews and as a psychologist is that really looking at and working on our relationships is not easy. Although almost everyone can describe outdoor situations in which relationship problems occurred, the prospect of addressing those problems directly is surprisingly daunting. I have spoken with world-class climbers, kayakers, and others who confront death in their sports but are much less sanguine about confronting relationship issues with their partners.

Just as fear or resistance to change can interfere with our ability to learn new outdoor skills, such feelings can also interfere with our ability to learn about and develop new relationship skills. As you read this book and think about your relationships, understand that it is normal to feel frustrated and perhaps anxious about the possibility of change. You may also have doubts about whether the suggestions in the book will work in your situation.

If you have those feelings, you may want to ask yourself if you haven't had similar doubts or anxieties when you learned other outdoor skills. For example, when you first ride a racing or mountain bike, does it feel natural to keep the high pedaling cadences that you are told are more efficient but that seem uncomfortable initially? Or when learning to ski, does it make sense or feel safe (in spite of what your instructor assures you) to lean down the hill on steep slopes?

To make progress, we often have to do things that initially feel uncomfortable or awkward. Just because something is unfamiliar doesn't mean it's wrong, and just because we've always done things a certain way does not mean our habitual patterns work well for us. With practice, new techniques eventually become second nature. To reach that stage, we must live with the awkwardness of trying something new and we should not expect perfect results on the first attempt.

Begin this book by recognizing that problems can and will arise in all partnerships, families, and groups, but they do not have to be disastrous. If you become aware that things are not going well, think of that as an opportunity to work on yourself and your relationships to make them better. This change in perspective is perhaps the most important concept of this book. It helps us transform even some of the most unpleasant experiences into vehicles for learning and change in ourselves and our relationships. Rather than simply getting mad or frustrated, we can realize what is happening, take a few deep breaths, and say, "Okay, so here's a problem. How are we going to understand each other and deal with things more effectively together so we can have fun?"

WHO THIS BOOK IS FOR

This book is written for couples, families, and groups who enjoy the outdoors together. Much of what is said applies equally well to each type of relationship, but a few preliminary comments should be made about wording and some things to keep in mind as you read.

A WORD ABOUT WORDS

To avoid gender stereotypes about men and women, I made a conscious effort to use neutral names and initials in examples and other descriptions or to balance the roles filled by men and women. I also wanted to make the book inclusive of all types of relationships. Although heterosexual couples predominate in our society, people in same-sex relationships face very similar challenges in combining their love for each other with their love for nature.

I use the terms "people" or "partners" to signify anyone with whom we might participate in outdoor activities. In a very real sense, when we venture outdoors with others, they become our partners. Partners can include significant others, spouses, family members, friends, group members, and anyone else who might be along. In our relationships with others and in our relationship with nature, thinking of the other as a partner enhances both our cooperation and our enjoyment.

COUPLES

When I interviewed people for this book, some couples said the best times they have together are when they are doing things outdoors. On the other hand, the most frequently expressed concerns and stories of conflict came from couples. For a variety of reasons, many couples seem to have difficulty balancing relationship issues with their outdoor pursuits.

For most couples, the best way to use this book is for both people to read and discuss it together. As you go through this book with your partner, you will find a number of checklists and exercises to facilitate exploration and discussion. One way to use these is for each of you to complete an exercise individually, then talk about your responses. Another useful technique is for each person to highlight portions of the book that seem particularly relevant, then discuss those sections together. If you use this approach, try to avoid the temptation to play "gotcha" by underlining everything you think is wrong with the other person and nothing that applies to yourself. I once worked with a couple in which each person came in to say how accurately a book about improving a marriage had described the problems the partner was having. It works much better to look at how *we* can change as well as how our partners can change.

In couples where one member is not interested in reading this book or trying other ways of making things better, the process is more difficult. One useful first step might be to invite the person who seems resistant to reflect on the quotes at the beginning of this chapter: "If we are not having fun, something needs to change." It is hard to argue with the simple truth of this statement. A person not wanting to deal with relationship issues usually has unexpressed reasons, but those reasons need to be voiced and discussed. Simply wishing things would be different won't solve problems any more than wishing it wouldn't rain will keep you dry.

If you are in a relationship in which you feel things aren't going well but your partner is not willing to work with you, this book may help you have a better understanding of where some of the problems are and how to deal with them. You may also want to explore chapter 10, Communication for Outdoor Partners, for ways of encouraging your partner to become more involved. If things still don't get any better in the relationship with your partner, the appendix at the back of the book deals with getting more help for your relationship.

FAMILIES

Many parents and children feel awkward talking about relationships and how they affect outdoor activities. In spite of this discomfort, talking about relationships within a family could go a long way toward helping children deal more successfully with conflicts as adults. If children grow up in families that recognize the importance of working constructively on relationship issues, they will come to value the process and will know how to participate with partners when they are older. Indeed, one of the reasons it feels awkward for adults to discuss relationship issues with our partners or children is that most of us never had such discussions in our own families when we were young.

In using this book with your family, keep in mind the importance of developmental differences in physical, mental, and emotional processes. To appreciate this, take a moment to consider how five-year-olds differ from ten-year-olds, or how ten-year-olds differ from fifteen-year-olds, in how they think and show emotions, or in their physical abilities. Do your best to recognize and understand such differences so you can adjust your activities and interactions to take into account each person's needs. This advice may seem obvious, but it is surprising how easily we forget that children think differently and have different physical abilities and emotional needs than adults.

One other note about families: When I speak of "families" in this book, I am referring to not just the "traditional" two-parent family but to any group of people that considers itself to be a family. For convenience I use the plural "parents" to refer broadly to the adult members of a family, whether they are single parents; pairs; step, adoptive, or biological parents; or other adults who are charged with the responsibility of caring for children.

GROUPS AND OUTDOOR ORGANIZATIONS

Talking about relationship issues with friends or members of an outdoor organization can be a very interesting experience. When I first raise this topic with informal groups of friends or with established organizations, the initial responses range from skeptically raised eyebrows to outright criticism. At the same time, however, members of every group I speak to can recount numerous incidents in which relationship problems ruined an outing or made an already challenging situation worse. In spite of group members' doubts, such experiences generally convince people to give this process a chance.

One way to increase a group's willingness to consider relationship issues is to point out that no one thinks it odd for a group leader to assess the experience and skill levels of a group or to complete an equipment checklist before an outing. One can then ask if the psychological makeup of the group is any less essential than their technical experience or equipment. Indeed, could anything be more important?

This explanation usually elicits at least agreement in principle, but many people will still be concerned about two issues. First, group members may fear they are being asked to be "psychoanalyzed" or to reveal some personal feelings that they would rather not share. This concern is perfectly reasonable and should be respected, but asking people to talk about their concerns before a trip, to be open about their level of actual experience, or even to talk directly about how they are feeling about a person or event is far from psychoanalysis.

The second fear of group members is a concern that if people talk about their relationships, hard feelings are likely to be created and the group may be threatened as a result. This fear is also understandable. There have no doubt been times when group members inwardly wanted to tear the hair off one another but everyone refrained and "had a good time" instead. On the other hand, there are probably at least as many occasions in which open conflicts in groups developed because people did not deal with issues directly and the underlying tensions spilled out in other ways and spoiled the activity.

Talking about relationships in a group before or during an activity may reveal tensions, but it is unlikely to create tensions where none existed before. The advantage is that by speaking directly and openly about how people are feeling, the group has a chance to deal with conflicts early and prevent them from escalating.

HOW TO USE THIS BOOK

Like every good outdoor guide, this book describes where to go, hazards to watch for along the way, and the things to bring along. Chapter 1, The Myth of "Perfect Relationships," explores the myth of ideal relationships and the causes of "relationship accidents." This chapter then introduces the "Relationship Ten Essentials"—qualities that everyone should carry with them in the outdoors.

Clarifying and sharing responsibilities, leaving other stresses behind, and escaping the roles of "the hurrier" and "the hurried" are addressed in chapter 2, Planning and Preparation. Chapter 3, Experience, considers how differences in experience are among the most common causes of relationship accidents and describes how they can be dealt with more successfully in the planning stage of activities. In chapter 4, Physical Preparation, the message is that we need not all be specimens of optimal fitness, but we do need to be realistic about what we and our partners can do and still have a good time. Chapter 5, Equipment, explains the value of having the right equipment and knowing how to use it. This chapter describes the relationship problems that result when equipment is not considered or when partners have equipment that differs in quality or malfunctions in the field. As a final step before setting out, chapter 6, Reasons for Being Outdoors Together, explores how we can keep our energy and focus on the relationship and having fun.

Chapter 7, On the Trail, deals with such things as physical demands, fear, competition, physical intimacy, and hygiene. Chapter 8, Teaching and Learning with Partners, focuses on what happens when partners become teachers or students of one another. Chapter 9, Men and Women, raises the admittedly risky but extremely important subject of differences and similarities between men and women. Roles and stereotypes, physical differences, communication styles, and other topics are considered here. Chapter 10, Communication for Outdoor

Partners, looks at ways in which communication can break down and describes how partners can work together to communicate more effectively.

Finally, the book concludes with a brief summary and an appendix, Getting Help, for people who might be considering therapy as a way to further enhance their relationships.

REDEFINING EXCELLENCE AND "PUTTING UP NEW ROUTES"

Excellence in outdoor activities can be defined as "the ability to perform with grace under difficult conditions." In climbing, the mark of excellence is to "put up new routes," to climb what has never been climbed before or via an approach that previously has not been done. In relationships, we need a different standard of quality.

Each time we venture outdoors we have the opportunity to achieve new "personal routes." These are not measured by a scale of technical difficulty and they will never be written up in magazines. Instead, they are quiet, personal achievements. The new routes in relationships consist of subtle changes in the ways we speak or act toward one another, in how we feel inside when we are together. The more difficult the situation and the more we are able to maintain ourselves and our relationships in harmony, the more we will have achieved another step toward excellence.

By forging new routes in our own lives and in the ways we relate to others, we not only enhance the outdoor experience and our personal relationships, we are also part of a larger process that must take place if our species is ever to find peace within itself and with nature.

THE MYTH OF "PERFECT RELATIONSHIPS"

"Let's just say it looked a whole lot easier in the guidebook."

"I always thought my Prince Charming would come in hiking boots.
I got the boots all right, but charm . . . we're still working on that."

WHEN WE THINK ABOUT ENJOYING THE OUTDOORS with other people, most of us have a fantasy of what the ideal experience would be like. For couples, the vision might be of the "perfect relationship," a couple so involved and in love with each other that they feel only complete acceptance and love. "Perfect couples" never argue or fight. On mountain hikes they lay together beside sparkling streams, the sun shines warmly, wild berries grow in abundance, birds sing in the trees, and deer feed peacefully in the meadow.

Less romantic but equally idyllic, the "perfect outdoor family" has children who never get tired or cold, never whine, and always appreciate learning and marveling about the beauty of nature. The "perfect parents" (who of course began their family as the "perfect couple") are always cheerful, patient, and understanding with each other and the children. They never bring work or other problems along on the trip and they are knowledgeable and competent in everything they do.

Then there are "perfect groups." Planning and traveling together in a celebration of cooperation, each person in the group does his or her fair share of the work and everyone is sensitive to everyone's needs. With no great differences in strength, abilities, experience, or goals, everyone shares in the same adventures and goes at the same pace, and no one feels left out or held back. Any problems are dealt with quickly, openly, and amicably, and hard feelings never develop.

WHY RELATIONSHIPS AND THE OUTDOORS DON'T ALWAYS GO TOGETHER

In spite of, or perhaps because of, our idyllic fantasies, many people find that conflicts seem most likely to happen when they are doing the very things they most enjoy with the people they care for most. This is especially frustrating and confusing because it is exactly the opposite of what we imagine and hope will happen. In our fantasy relationships, we do not need to know how to deal with conflict because conflict never develops.

But reality is not so simple.

If we think for a moment, it should not be surprising that the reality of outdoor experiences so often clashes with the fantasy. When we first learn to hike, camp, ski, climb, canoe, or do any other outdoor sport, it makes sense to take a class, go with an experienced friend, or at least read a book before starting out. As we develop new skills that we know take time and practice to learn, we expect there to be falls.

Even when we consider ourselves accomplished, there are always new challenges and discoveries. All this we take for granted. But when it comes to our relationships, things are different.

Most people who combine relationships with their enjoyment of outdoor sports give almost no thought, training, or preparation to taking care of the relationship itself. We are willing to pay the price in both time and money for lessons and equipment to learn a new activity, but we resist conscious thought or attention to how we interact with each other. It is as if we believe what happens between people should just take care of itself without training, effort, or practice.

Sure it should. And on the first day, with no previous experience or training, we should all be able to ski double-diamond slopes, hike twenty miles, kayak Class IV water, run a marathon, ride a century bike ride, climb 5.10 rock, and windsurf the Columbia Gorge at thirty knots. No problem.

In many of the sports just mentioned, the consequences of ignorance and poor preparation is humiliation if you are lucky, significant injury or worse if you are not. In the case of relationships, poor preparation is no less dangerous. At the very least you can expect disappointment, hurt feelings, anger, and, sometimes, entirely losing the joy of the activity or the relationship itself. Worse still, in some situations, relationship conflicts have led to serious accidents and sometimes deaths.

THE RELATIONSHIP ACCIDENT REPORT

In an effort to increase the safety of sports such as climbing, kayaking, skiing, etc., participants have formed committees that investigate the causes of accidents. Reports of these investigations are published each year, and for those involved in the sports they make for rather macabre yet informative reading.

A distinguishing feature of accident reports is their telegraphic style and a perspective that reads as if some distant observer watched the whole thing develop and took note of what was happening. Most reports are introduced by subheadings that summarize the incident. An example might be: "Mount Anywhere, April 17, 1995—Inadequate equipment, lost route, uncontrolled slide down forty-five–degree snow-field ending in rocks. One death, one head injury, one broken arm."

Cheery, these are not. But they do serve a purpose. By studying how things have gone wrong for others, we may be able to avoid similar accidents ourselves. Although there are no safety committees to evaluate how things can go wrong in outdoor relationships, a typical "relationship accident" report might sound like this:

Accident #1: "First backpacking trip together—engagement canceled"

Background: KR—10 years' backpacking experience, JP—minimal previous experience; couple together 10 months, engaged to be married; KR planned hike of 3 days, 22 miles round trip, 6,000 feet total elevation gain, JP had no input in planning; KR's equipment state of the art, JP purchased new boots, borrowed or rented remaining equipment

Day 1: Work demands for both and long drive delayed start until late afternoon; weather cloudy, rain predicted; early pace too fast but interrupted by frequent stops to adjust JP's equipment; KR visibly impatient; blisters developed quickly for JP but left untreated; weather worsened—first drizzle, then hard rain as darkness fell; unable to reach planned campsite, makeshift camp established at 3 miles; dinner—hard rolls, cheese, trail mix; JP's clothing and sleeping bag wet; temperature dropped during night; no romance

Day 2: Still raining; couple considered abandoning plans and returning early—JP wanted nothing more, but was afraid to disappoint KR and insisted on going on; weather stayed bad, trail muddy; JP's blisters opened, KR frustrated, put moleskin on blisters; slippery log bridge across creek frightened JP; couple began to fight; at 10:30 A.M., 6 miles, and 2,000 feet, couple turned back; on return, KR slipped on wet stump and sprained ankle, blamed JP for cause of accident (if they hadn't turned back, KR wouldn't have slipped)— injury slowed the pace further; did not reach car till late afternoon, spoke very little during drive home, and did not return home until dark

Two weeks later: Engagement canceled

This report is imaginary, but it contains many of the ingredients common to outdoor relationship accidents: differences in needs, goals, experience, preparation, equipment, physical ability, fear, discomfort, and natural conditions. Differences in personalities and styles of interacting also contribute to the conflict, as do the influence of stresses from work, home, and other activities that are unrelated to the activity itself. Adding to the difficulties is the fact that once problems have developed, most people do not have effective ways of coping with them, communicating, or resolving conflicts.

With so many things that can go wrong, it may seem a wonder that people even attempt to do outdoor activities together. Precisely this sentiment was voiced by a friend who said, "On the first page of a relationship guidebook I'd write something like 'How to do things together in the outdoors without having a fight.' Then, when you turn the page it would say 'Forget it. It can't be done. The end.' It'll sell like hotcakes." Another person I spoke with said it somewhat differently: "If they can put a man on the moon, why can't Bob and I even hike to the Alpine Lakes without screaming at each other?"

Getting along with each other while doing outdoor activities can be a vexing problem. Fortunately, by approaching the problem in steps and learning from others, it is possible to do what sometimes seems beyond the reach of mere mortals. People can actually learn to get along and even have fun together. One key to making this happen is to remember the "Relationship Ten Essentials," the essential qualities for successful outdoor relationships.

WHO YOU ARE AND WHAT TO BRING

Anyone who has read a guidebook or taken a course from The Mountaineers is well versed in their "Ten Essentials." This is a list of items that should be taken on every outdoor activity: map, compass, flashlight/headlamp with spare bulbs and batteries, extra food, extra clothing, sunglasses, first-aid supplies, pocket knife, matches in waterproof container, and fire starter.

In contrast to the original Ten Essentials, the "Relationship Ten Essentials" identifies the personal qualities and skills we need to cope with both the human and the natural challenges of being outdoors together. The list was developed by asking people to name the characteristics they consider most important to making outdoor relationships work.

As with the original Ten Essentials, the Relationship Ten Essentials are best thought of as required elements, things every member should bring along on every trip. The most technically accomplished, physically fit, and well-equipped people can easily turn a wonderful outing into a miserable experience if they do not attend at least as much to their relationships as they do to their equipment and technique. Just as it's inviting trouble to say, "I don't think we'll need to start a fire so I'm not taking any matches," relationship problems are likely to happen when we say, "I like things done my way and if I have to change, forget it." When we refuse to carry matches, we run the risk of spending a long, cold night. When we refuse to be flexible in our relationships, we run the risk of spending a long, cold life.

RELATIONSHIP TEN ESSENTIALS

- Self-Awareness—knowledge of our own personality, wants, needs, abilities, quirks, and strengths, and an appreciation for how these influence our partners
- Flexibility—the willingness and ability to change plans or activities in response to natural conditions or the needs of partners
- Curiosity and a desire to learn—openness to new experiences and new ways of doing things in the outdoors; an attitude that finds something interesting in every environment and an opportunity to learn in every activity
- Patience—accepting the fact that some things take time and people move at different paces; being willing to give ourselves and our partners time to change
- Cooperation—the ability to work together toward common goals and to say "we did it" when the goals are achieved
- Sensitivity—the ability to appreciate, respect, and empathize with the needs and experience of our partners
- Trust—relying on one another to work together, make the best of whatever comes along, and, most importantly, keep the quality of the relationship a top priority
- Communication—expressing our own thoughts and feelings and really listening to, respecting, and understanding the ideas and feelings of our partners
- Humor—the ability to laugh at ourselves and with our partners and to find the lighter side of even the most trying conditions
- Love and respect for nature—meeting nature on nature's terms, honoring the beauty as well as the hardship, learning the lessons, accepting the strength and joy, and preserving the mystery

The chapters that follow explore the most common sources of conflict in outdoor relationships and describe how they can be managed constructively. Regardless of the specific problem or solution, the

Relationship Ten Essentials provide a background that applies to whatever comes up in the outdoors. If everyone carries this list in their mind and does their best to carry it out in their actions, outdoor relationships are sure to improve.

CHAPTER 2

PLANNING AND PREPARATION

*"If you want to know the truth,
most of the time problems start before we even get in the car to go."*

*"I realize now that I had no idea what I was getting into.
If I had it to do over again, I never would have gone
on such a difficult trip as that."*

THE BEST WAY TO DEAL WITH ACCIDENTS IN THE OUTDOORS is to prevent them. The same rule applies to relationship accidents, but a surprising number of conflicts arise before people actually reach the outdoors. Relationship problems often start and are sometimes at their worst when people are getting ready to go on outdoor trips. After relationship or other accidents occur, people then look back and, in hindsight, see clearly that the roots of the problems lay in what took place or should have taken place during the preparation stage.

This chapter is about how preparation can enhance the enjoyment of relationships and outdoor adventures. The chapter begins by describing the familiar roles of "hurrier" and "hurried" and how these relate to conflicts in preparation. This is followed by suggestions for how disputes about getting started can be resolved more successfully for couples, families, and groups. Because conflicts at the end of outings are almost as frequent as conflicts before, the discussion of planning also covers who takes care of the after-trip details.

To help make sure everything is taken care of during planning, a checklist is provided that reviews logistical details, equipment, information, and relationship issues. Finally, because many conflicts that on the surface appear to be about preparation are actually related to underlying issues, the chapter concludes by exploring how we can identify those issues and how the connection between vacation time and conflict time can be changed.

GETTING READY ON TIME
THE "HURRIERS" VERSUS THE "HURRIED"

Ask almost any couple or family, and they can tell you without hesitation who fills the roles of the "hurrier" and the "hurried." They may also say that arguments between "hurriers" and "hurried" are a regular part of preparing for the outdoors.

"Hurriers" are the people who take it upon themselves to get everyone else ready on time. Typical "hurrier" behaviors usually begin several days ahead of the actual departure date. Statements like "we don't want to be late on Friday" or "let's try to get an early start" let people know the hurrier is already thinking about time. As the departure nears, hurriers exude an almost palpable sense of urgency. They look at their watches every few minutes and make frequent checks to see how everyone is doing. When the planned time inevitably passes without everyone ready, hurriers show still greater signs of tension.

Drumming fingers, sulking in a chair, criticism, slammed doors, and words that really "should not be used in front of the children" all attest to the hurrier's frustrations.

Some hurriers simply prefer to be on time no matter what they do, but in outdoor relationships hurriers are often driven by specific concerns or desires. For example, hurriers may be concerned that late starts are dangerous. Weather conditions may change, planned routes are less safe at certain times, and late starts can mean late and possibly dangerous after-dark returns. Hurriers may also have personal preferences for being early. "Beating crowds," getting first tracks on fresh snow, finding good campsites, or other valid reasons can add to the hurrier's desires and pressure to get underway.

Partners of "hurriers" become the "hurried." Some who fill the role of the "hurried" simply do not share the same sense of urgency as their "hurrier" partners. They prefer a more leisurely pace and feel that if they have to be "so uptight" all the time, it isn't worth it. When hurriers begin to get apoplectic, this type of hurrieds are likely to say something like "relax, we'll get there on time" or "the mountain will still be there, what's the rush?"

A second type of "hurrieds" shares a concern about time and works as quickly as they can, but they still feel pressured to go even faster. In spite of their best efforts, hurrieds of this type repeatedly are made aware that they are somehow letting down or angering their partners. As the hurriers race about telling everyone to get going, the hurrieds resent the added pressure and are likely to become angry themselves.

If the pressure between the hurriers and hurried becomes too great, both may wish they were not going at all or at least that they were not going together. This is clearly not the best way to start a trip. On the other hand, there must be something to it because so many people go through the same sort of ritual every time they go places. One couple I spoke with had been married almost thirty years but said they played out the same scenario whether they were going camping, on vacation, or even just to the movies. As we talked about the pattern, one of them paused and said, "We could have saved a lot of hurt feelings for both of us if we'd found a better way to do it."

AVOIDING THE TIME CRUNCH

Fortunately, it is possible to avoid these kinds of conflicts. In contrast to the couple that had been struggling for years, another couple shared a solution that worked quite well for them and might for others as well.

"We used to leave everything till the last minute," one partner commented. "That always created problems because there was so much pressure and we always seemed to forget something or show up late and have everyone waiting for us. I can't tell you how many fights that caused. Now we try to pack at a least whole day in advance and have it all sitting there ready to go. That way we're not running around like maniacs at the last minute. We have time to talk, and we don't leave things behind in the rush. If we do start arguing about something as we get ready, we at least get the argument out of the way a day early so we can settle it and feel good about each other when we actually leave."

Another way to reduce conflicts related to rushed departures is to be more realistic about how much time it takes to get ready. When sufficient time is allowed for preparation, the roles of hurrier and hurried become less important and less emotionally charged. Although I have been hiking and climbing for years, I realized only recently that it often takes me much longer than I thought to get my pack and other gear ready. I can recall times when I said something like, "Don't worry, it should only take about an hour or so to get everything ready and loaded. We can easily go to the show, pack when we get back, and still be in bed by 10:30 or 11:00." Inevitably, as we discovered we were out of trail mix, or pairs of hiking socks turned out to be missing, or countless other delays appeared, the eleven o'clock bedtime gradually became midnight, then one and later, until we at last went to bed dreading the 5:30 alarm ahead. After countless such experiences, I have come to accept that it usually takes about two and sometimes as much as three times as long as my optimistic estimates to really have everything ready to go.

FAMILIES AND PREPARATION TIME

The difference between estimated and actual preparation time becomes even greater when families get ready for an outdoor adventure. A weary mother confided, "I hate to say it, but when the family is going together on an outing, it probably takes—or at least it feels like it takes—four to five times longer than I want it to. Sometimes it seems like we won't get out of the house at all until it's already time to be back."

Families take longer to prepare for a variety of reasons. There are more things needed to get ready: more food to prepare, more gear to load, more individual needs to take into consideration. More people and more equipment also means more possibilities for things to go wrong: more pairs of socks to find, more pieces of equipment that might be broken or lost, etc. Then there are issues such as everyone trying to get into the bathroom at the same time, squabbles over who sits where in the car, and all the other conflicts that normally happen in families.

Family preparations also take longer because children may not know exactly what they need to bring along or how they should get things together. One way to deal with this is to go through a preparation checklist with the children so they know what to expect and what they will need for an activity. If children feel they are part of the planning process, understand what is happening, and have a role to play, they are more likely to contribute and participate.

With older teens, you may want to use the checklist presented later in the chapter. For younger children, a simplified version is usually easier. Children's lists should include just the immediate things they will need for themselves. The right kinds of shoes, socks, warm clothes, backpack, etc., should be the main items on a child's list. As children grow older, an added sense of responsibility can be fostered by including group needs and emphasizing the importance of bringing these things along for the whole family.

Allowing sufficient time by preparing a couple of days in advance can be especially helpful with children. Getting things ready in advance reduces last-minute delays and helps build enthusiasm for the upcoming adventure. One little girl proudly invited me into her room to show me her already prepared backpack. It was all set for a weekend hike that was still two days away. She also went over her personal equipment checklist and showed me where everything was in her pack. When the time came for her family to leave, it would be easy to simply load the already packed backpack and head out. This family had found a way for the children to participate, feel pride and responsibility, and be under way on time.

WHO PREPARES WHAT

Another contributing factor in pre-trip conflicts is that people are often involved in different aspects of preparation and may not fully appreciate what their partners are doing. For example, if a couple is preparing for a canoe trip, one person may be in charge of putting the canoe on the car and loading the rest of the canoeing equipment. Meanwhile, the other person may be getting together food and clothing, making sure the cooking gear and eating utensils are clean, and taking care of last-minute details around the house.

On the surface, this sounds like an effective division of labor. Both sets of activities are essential and must be accomplished for the trip to proceed. But as people go about their own tasks, they may not be aware of all that their partner is doing. When one person finishes his or her part of the preparation, it is easy to think everything else should be ready. This situation is tailor-made for "hurriers." Once they have finished their primary task, hurriers are free to direct their energies to pressuring everyone else to move faster.

This pattern is frequently a source of conflict for couples, but it is almost universally an issue for families. A common scenario is for one parent to be concerned with getting the equipment ready while the other is involved with getting the people ready. Often, though not always, it is the dad who deals with equipment and the mom who deals with the kids. When dad has the equipment set but mom is still struggling to help the kids get dressed, pack their lunches, and bring along pillows, books, and all the other things kids need but dads can do without, dads tend to get frustrated and start their "hurrier" routine. Mom, who has been doing her best and has been dealing with her own set of stresses, is none too happy at being asked, "What's taking so long?"

Part of the problem in these circumstances is that the partners are not really working as partners. Instead, each is doing things separately, not fully realizing what the other is doing or the time and effort it requires. One couple addressed this issue by trading roles for their next few trips. The experience was enlightening for both.

"I was amazed at how much work it is just to get all the kids ready to go," the dad remarked. "One minute I'd be trying to get the food ready, the next minute one of the kids would need help with something, and before I could get back to the food some other crisis had come up that I had to deal with. When Pat came in and said everything was all set, I started to get angry with her and with the kids."

Meanwhile, the mom, who changed roles and was now dealing with equipment, said, "It's not easy to get the boat on the roof all by yourself. It's really awkward. I smashed my thumb trying to keep it from falling off the rack. Then it took awhile to find and sort out all the rest of the equipment and be sure we had everything. Checking the car out also took more time than I thought. It turned out we were low on oil and I had to add that. Then the tires needed air and I had to get them filled. After I'd done all that and everyone else still wasn't ready, I found myself getting cranky."

Following this experience, this couple sat down together and tried to estimate more realistically how much time it took them to do all that was necessary. They also talked about how each could help the other and work together as a team. In the process, they agreed that for them it would probably work better if they both loaded the gear first, then both worked to help the kids get ready. That way, each knew what the other was doing and was there to help out if problems arose. This solution also reduced the tendency for one person to finish tasks more quickly and be left waiting impatiently for the other.

Another couple took a somewhat different approach that worked well for them. This couple realized that one person simply moved more slowly and had more personal things to take care of in preparation. If both started at the same time to take care of the things they had to do, the faster one was bound to finish first and then become irritated at having to wait for the other. They discovered two ways of dealing with this. Sometimes the slower person would start to get ready well before the faster partner. This allowed one to have sufficient time to prepare while the other either stayed in bed a little longer or read the paper. The alternative solution was for both to start preparing at the same time and then, when one was ready, rather than waiting impatiently or trying to hurry the other, the person who was ready could read, rest, or do something else during the available time. This couple found that as long as they both understood, agreed upon, and held to a set time to leave, it really didn't matter that one could prepare faster than the other.

COPING WITH THE HABITUALLY LATE IN GROUPS

With a little effort, most couples and families can sit down together and agree on how they can best be ready in time for a given activity. The situation is somewhat more complicated with groups because each participant depends on all the others to do whatever is necessary to be ready and present on time. Unfortunately, in many groups, a few people can be counted on to be late or unprepared.

The first thing to ask about these situations is, "Has anyone talked to these folks and told them exactly what time departure is and that it is important to be on time?" It sometimes happens that people sincerely do not know it upsets others when they are late. In most cases, when this is explained, the individuals are willing and able to change and they soon begin arriving slightly early rather than late.

Another approach to habitual lateness may be to offer those who are late some of the suggestions presented earlier in this chapter. For example, the idea of getting things ready the day before might be useful for some. Others might benefit from using the preparation and equipment checklist offered later in this chapter. I once gave friends a copy of the checklist and they were sincerely appreciative. As they arrived on time for the next trip, they thanked me and said they didn't know why they hadn't used something like that before.

If speaking directly and offering suggestions fail to bring people on time, a less direct approach is to estimate the average amount of time certain people are usually late, then tell those people a departure time that is a corresponding amount of time earlier than the departure time told to more reliably punctual group members. This doesn't really help those people understand the punctuality situation, but at least those who arrive on time don't have to wait for them as long.

A more draconian but sometimes necessary measure, which can be particularly important for large groups, is to establish an agreement that the departure time means precisely that: the time at which people actually leave from the meeting point to go on the activity. The clear and unmistakable message should be that, at the departure time, the bikes, cars, bus, or other transportation leaves and those who are not on board will not be going with the group.

People may not feel comfortable about leaving at the designated time if everyone has not arrived, but it can be even more uncomfortable for a large group of people to be detained because a few are habitually late. Experience suggests that when the expectation is clearly set and consistently followed through, those who are late quickly learn to adapt or they cease to participate. Either way, it is their choice and others are not consistently put out or delayed by their actions.

If you do plan to hold firmly to a set departure time, it is very important to be clear about that fact. Unless it is specified, "departure" time is often interpreted to mean "meeting time," which then means that even if everyone arrives at that time, there will be still further delays as gear is prepared, people chat, equipment is loaded, etc. To deal with this, group members can be informed that they should arrive sufficiently in advance of the departure time to unload and load gear and to allow for whatever unforeseen circumstances might delay their arrival.

Again, it is important to be realistic. It is not at all uncommon for hikers to arrive on time at the trailhead, then take as long as an hour to work on their equipment, use the bathroom, realize they need to wear different clothes, use the bathroom again, work some more on their gear, use the bathroom one more time, and finally be set to leave.

In addition to being clear about the departure time, it is also helpful to be sure people who will be driving have a full tank of gas when they arrive at the meeting point. Merely being at the location on time does not solve the problems if the caravan of cars then has to follow one to a gas station and wait in line until that person is actually ready to leave.

If people will be ride-sharing or carpooling, part of the advance planning might also be to notify everyone of the expected contribution each person should make for gas and other expenses. Many parties include one or two people who somehow, usually unintentionally, never remember or have cash on hand to chip in for gas. This is unfair to the drivers and eventually leads to hard feelings. Such feelings are typically left unvoiced, because the driver feels he or she should not have to tell people, they should just know to pay their share. One way to ensure they know is to tell them in advance. That may seem tacky to some, but it beats holding bad feelings inside.

Another common cause of lateness and delays in groups is that people do not receive clear instructions for getting to the meeting point or the point at which the actual activity starts. Assuming that everyone knows the place or offering complex verbal directions instead of writing things down is almost sure to cause delays and frustration. It is always worth the time to be sure that everyone has a map or unmistakable written instructions for both how to get to the meeting point and how to get from there to the destination.

PLANNING FOR NORMAL AND LATE RETURN TIMES

In the excitement and stress of preparing to leave for a trip, it is easy to pay less attention to when and how one plans to return. This can lead to serious problems if people fail to return on time. If return times and procedures are not addressed in advance, friends or family members will begin to worry and may not know what to do. Many costly and dangerous rescue efforts have been mounted unnecessarily because people failed to make clear plans for when they would return and what should be done if they were late. To prevent this, each member of the couple, family, or group should know when the expected return time is, what kind of time "window" is reasonable for the trip to run longer than expected, what problems this could create for members, and what should be done if a party is overdue to return.

Failure to be clear about return times and possible extensions is particularly likely to create problems if some participants have made plans based on inaccurate or misunderstood information. I was with a group about halfway into a river trip when one of the members looked at his watch and asked how soon we would be finished. He and his wife were supposed to meet someone in an hour, but there were still at least four hours to go before we reached the takeout point. Much of the remainder of the trip was spent listening to the couple worry aloud over the missed appointment and carp at each other for the error.

In this situation, no one had actually told the couple, and they had not thought to ask, how long the trip would be. They simply assumed it would be brief and made plans accordingly. The easiest way to avoid this would obviously have been to check and be sure everyone knew the estimated time of return.

DEALING WITH LATE RETURNS
A different sort of problem also occurs with regularity in the outdoors. Whatever plans one may make for the probable time to complete an activity, nature is unpredictable and myriad things can cause delays. Injuries, losing the trail, bad weather, fatigue, equipment malfunctions, and any number of other minor or major calamities can easily add hours to a planned arrival. The solution to this is to allow for such occurrences and learn to overestimate how long you think the outing will take. Finishing a trip a little early rarely upsets people, but coming in well past the predicted time can be demoralizing and possibly dangerous. Experienced outdoorspeople often follow a practice of estimating a likely time of arrival, adding a proportionate amount of time to that as a fudge factor, then adding still more time as a safety margin.

Correctly estimating the time and allowing for a safety margin not only helps prevent conflict among those who are doing the activity together, it also reduces conflicts between those who went on the activity and any significant others who stayed home. Waiting for someone to return who is overdue in the outdoors can be incredibly nerve-wracking for partners at home.

The wife of an avid kayaker said that on many evenings she found herself anxiously waiting for her husband to return. As he became more and more overdue, she felt a familiar growing dread at the possibility that he might have been trapped and drowned. She also became angry because this was a regular occurrence and her husband never seemed to appreciate what it put her through when he was late. Describing this mix of feelings, she said, "I can't tell you how many nights I've sat home just listening for that car to pull up and saying to myself that if he's drowned I'll never forgive him, and if he hasn't drowned and is putting me through this for nothing, I'll kill him."

Another couple had experienced similar difficulties until it happened that the partner who was usually the one left at home waiting went on a rather dangerous rafting trip without her spouse. The raft trip went without a hitch, but afterwards everyone celebrated by having pizza together at a tavern near the river. The woman tried calling home to tell her husband she would be late, but the line was busy and she did not get through. Meanwhile, her husband, who had never been in this situation before, was growing increasingly angry and frantic (exactly what his wife had been feeling all those years). By the time his wife did arrive home, he had called the sheriff and the search-and-rescue team was just about to launch a search of the river. After a rather heated exchange, the wife apologized for the concern she had caused and her husband was at last able to appreciate what she had been telling him for many years.

This couple's experience also raises another consideration. Beyond establishing a realistically conservative predicted return time, it is essential that someone who is not on the trip be notified of a specified time by which search or other procedures will be initiated. This time should be such that ordinary, or even extraordinary, delays would not take the party beyond it, but it is still sufficiently early that help could be sent in time to do some good if it were really needed.

How the critical time is established depends on such things as the experience level of the parties involved, their ability and preparedness to cope with unusual situations, and conditions such as the risks of the activity, weather conditions, etc. Whatever time is set, those on the activity must do absolutely everything in their power, short of exposing themselves to even greater risk, to get back by the designated time or at least somehow get word out that they are okay and people do not need to worry or send help.

Along with knowing the specified return time, those who are waiting should also know exactly what to do if that time is exceeded. It is a good practice to leave with a designated person a map of the planned route, estimated times at key locations along the route, and phone numbers of the appropriate search or rescue groups to contact. For group outings, someone who will not be on the trip should be designated as a coordinator and his or her name and number should be given to all the partners who are not along on the trip and might become concerned. The coordinator should have the names and numbers of those on the trip, as well as the names and numbers of people who should be called if there is an unexpected delay or a real emergency. If the coordinator receives word that everyone is okay but they will be later than expected, he or she can call everyone else and save a lot of people a lot of anxiety. If real problems have developed, having one person contact the necessary officials with the critical information can save a great deal of confusion and can help make coordinating searches or rescues much more effective.

PLANS FOR DE-RIGGING

Just as people often report that conflicts arise before an outdoor activity has begun, it is also common for conflicts to occur at the end of trips. One reason for this is that people do not include plans for "de-rigging" as part of their advance preparations. De-rigging is the process of taking care of all the equipment, clothing, and other gear after an outdoor activity is completed. Sufficient time for de-rigging should be included during the planning process and there should be discussion of who will do what part of the cleaning, repairing, or storing of the equipment.

Working together to take care of the equipment after a trip is important both as a way to preserve the equipment itself and to preserve the relationship among participants. Anyone who has left wet sleeping bags or tents in stuff sacks knows how hard it is to get rid of the mildew smell the next time you want to use them. Similarly, skis left in their ski bags will soon have rusty edges, as will crampons, ice axes, and other metal tools that are put away wet. Cooking gear has to be cleaned and put away for the next use, and clothing that is not washed, sorted, and stored in an organized way will invariably be lost when it is time for the next use.

The question for relationships is, who will do all of these things? At the end of an outdoor activity, people are usually tired and dirty. Everyone wants nothing more than a hot bath, and no one is really thrilled about dealing with all the muddy, smelly gear. That is precisely why it is important to work together so that no one feels they have to do all the "dirty work."

When groups of people go on outings, each person is generally responsible for de-rigging his or her own gear. If everyone used certain equipment in common, such as someone's raft, cooking gear, or vehicle, it is only fair to pitch in and help clean things up and put it away. The old phrase "many hands make light the work" is especially true when it comes to this part of an activity.

I had the opportunity once to work with a team of German kayakers and, as impressed as I was by their skill as kayakers and their knowledge of safety and rescue techniques, I remember also being struck by how efficiently and cooperatively everyone contributed to the de-rigging process. Because everyone knew what to do and how to help, as soon as we arrived home lines were set up for drying clothes, kayaks were taken off the vehicle and were quickly cleaned and put in storage, the van was swept and cleaned, and everything was put in its place in a remarkably short time. I asked one of the members about this and was told that they learn this part of kayaking at the same time they learn how to kayak. If the group works together, everything gets done quickly and right, then it's time to enjoy some beer together.

One of the reasons the German kayaking group worked so well together at de-rigging was that they learned it at an early age. Rather than treating the process as an unpleasantry to be avoided, this group taught the youth in their kayaking club that if they wanted to learn to kayak they had to also learn how to put things away properly at the end of the day.

In contrast to this group, parents in many families assume the responsibility for taking care of things after an activity is finished. While the parents do the work of putting everything away, the children are allowed to go inside, get cleaned up, and relax. Sometimes this might make sense, for example, if it is especially late and the children are exhausted, but in general I think it is important to involve children as much as possible in all aspects of the activity, including the parts that are not necessarily fun. By teaching this lesson early and giving children specific tasks that they are able and responsible to do, parents can create a cooperative atmosphere and at the same time teach a value that will serve the children well as they develop and go on to do activities on their own.

THE PLANNING PROCESS

To be sure that logistical details and relationship issues are addressed during preparation, it can be extremely helpful to follow a systematic approach. A useful tool to facilitate this is the planning process checklist provided later in this section.

This list focuses on the process of preparation and the critical details that must be attended to. The purpose is to make sure that partners talk about each aspect of preparation and the activity together. If the list is used well, before an activity gets underway everyone will be informed about and comfortable with what they will be doing, who will be participating, where and when they will be going and returning, what they will need to know and be able to do, what to bring and how to use it, and how the people involved will work together.

Ideally, the planning process checklist should be completed well before an outing begins. Couples and families should discuss the list together and group leaders should have a copy by their phone or in hand as they discuss the plans with each potential participant. For the list to work, each person should be involved in the planning process and should check off the portions of the list just as they would an equipment checklist. Simply checking items without really thinking about them or voicing any concerns would be as ineffective as checking an equipment list that said "tent" or "stove" when one had no idea how to put up the tent or how to fuel and light the stove. Checking an element of the list should mean each person knows and has carefully considered and discussed any ideas, concerns, issues, feelings, or other reactions and is comfortable with all elements of the activity as planned.

If a leader or other member of a group senses that someone is not fully in accord with or attentive to some item of the preparation checklist—for example, if a member declines to write down the directions to a new meeting site or if someone says "we'll be there around 7:30 A.M." when the departure time is *exactly* 7:30 A.M.—the importance of the issue should be stressed. The leader may also want to comment on the apparent indifference of the participant and consider carefully how that might affect the success of the outing. It is far better to risk a bit of offense during planning rather than to experience the frustration and anger that occur when a few people arrive unprepared or late and everyone else must wait.

This list is meant to serve as an overall review. Several items of the list, for example those referring to equipment, may require separate and more detailed lists to be prepared and reviewed for the specific activity. Those lists should also be carefully reviewed together with each participant.

PLANNING PROCESS CHECKLIST

Instructions: This list is designed to help partners work together to plan their outdoor activities. Each item of the list should be carefully reviewed with each person who will be participating in an activity. For certain items, specific details or additional information should be provided participants. Checking items on the list should signify that the information has been discussed with each participant and that each person is sufficiently informed and prepared.

Preparation Process, Departure Time and Place, and Return

- What pre-trip details, e.g., permits, registration, group communications, etc., must be attended to and who will take care of them. (Establish a process for verifying in advance that all such details have been completed.)
- The precise time and location of departure by vehicle and clear directions for how to get to the departure site. (Check with each person to be sure they know precisely where to go. Do not simply ask, "Do you know where that is?" Have each person describe how to get there. If needed, provide everyone with maps and directions.)
- Carpooling or other transportation arrangements. (Names, phone numbers, and directions must be shared with drivers and passengers. Clearly establish who will drive, who will be passengers, and how this will be coordinated. Also discuss the matter of sharing expenses.)

- The location of the start and finish of the activity itself and clear directions for precisely how to get there. (Do not simply ask if people know; have them describe clear directions for where to go and how to get there. Maps should be provided if needed.)
- The best estimate of return time, and what to do if return is late. (Identify someone as a coordinator who will manage things if the party is late to return. That person should have lists of all participants with names and numbers to contact if there is a late return. That person should also have an agreed-upon plan for what to do and should have a list of emergency contacts and phone numbers if needed.)
- "De-rigging" plans. (Names and specific responsibilities for de-rigging should be clarified in advance.)

Information about the Activity

- The level of physical demands required by the activity and the necessary physical preparation of each person. (Use specific details about length of trip, planned pace, and special physical challenges. As a reference, one can describe comparable other trips or similar activities that participants should be able to manage well in order to not only complete but also enjoy the planned outing. If someone is not up to the demands of an activity, perhaps that person should not go or the plans should be changed.)
- The degree of technical difficulty and skill required and the necessary preparation and experience of each person. (Clear information should be provided about the ratings and difficulty of the activity and the types and levels of skills required. Again, if the activity is beyond someone's abilities, either the plans should be changed, the person should chose a different trip, or some other arrangements should be made.)
- Any risks or dangers that might be encountered and how they will be dealt with. (This includes known generic hazards of the activity as well as the hazards of the specifically planned outing. These matters should be thoroughly addressed each time and one should not assume people know them. Do not assume that, because people say they have done similar things before, they know what the risks or demands of a specific activity or trip will be.)
- Likely weather conditions and how they will be dealt with. (This

should include reference to necessary gear, equipment for unexpected weather, and clear information about the possibility of canceling, postponing, or selecting a different destination, route, or activity.)

▪ Most likely or possible contingency plans in the event of difficulties. (Include advance agreement about how to deal with unexpected circumstances.)

Equipment

▪ All equipment, including food, hardware, clothing, etc., required for safety and enjoyment, and who will bring what personal and group equipment. (A separate checklist should be used to identify specific needs for a specific activity. Nothing on this list should be taken for granted and everyone should verify that they are bringing all the required items.)

▪ Knowledge of how to use and maintain equipment correctly and safely. (Ask each person specifically if there is any item of equipment he or she has not actually used more than once in a real outdoor situation. If the item will be needed, each person must know how to use it and have practice prior to the trip.)

▪ Inspection and pretesting or breaking in of new equipment. (Ask each person if there is any new equipment he or she has not tested. Be particularly attentive to footwear, packs, stoves, tents, safety equipment, or other hardware that is commonly associated with problems of fit, use, or function. If people have not yet broken in or tested equipment before a trip, they should either do so or reconsider participation until they have. Ask each person to inspect each piece of equipment to be sure everything is in good repair and working order.)

People

▪ Names of the people who will be going and information about their personalities, experience, and other qualities. (Briefly discuss the names, backgrounds, experience, skills, fitness, and other personal qualities of participants. Each person should have an idea of the other people who will be along. If there are any known concerns, these should be discussed openly beforehand so constructive solutions to problems can be developed or plans can be changed.)

▪ How decisions will be made among the partners. (Discuss decision-making processes that will be used on the trip. If there will be a leader, identify that leader. If different people will be responsible for different elements of the trip, e.g., route finding, setting up camp, safety, medical needs, etc., they should be identified in advance and all participants should know who will do what and why.)

Purpose for Doing the Activity Together

- How the activity was chosen. (Check to be sure that each person is personally interested in going on the activity as planned, with the people involved, and as described in detail by the items of this checklist. If people have mixed emotions about going, perhaps they should reconsider or plans should be adapted to address their concerns.)
- Individual and group goals. (Clarify what each person would want to happen during the activity in order to enjoy themselves and feel good about having participated.)

DEALING WITH UNDERLYING ISSUES

It is important to recognize that although the planning process checklist and other preparation strategies described in this chapter can go a long way toward reducing relationship accidents, problems may still arise. One reason for this is that many conflicts that appear to be about getting ready for the outdoors are really about underlying issues that have been present for some time but have not been directly addressed or resolved.

When people I interviewed talked about pre-trip relationship accidents, a typical pattern began to emerge. In this pattern, the partners are overworked and overstressed, and rarely have time to really talk with one another about their relationship. As a result, issues that have not been dealt with along the way have in effect been "saved up" for when there is more time. Unfortunately, the only time for those issues to emerge happens also to be the only time people have to get away outdoors together.

One woman put it this way: "I've noticed that there's a connection between how long it's been since we went on a trip and how long and serious the arguments are at the start of the next trip. What worries me is that each time we seem to get over the fight enough to have fun, but I don't think we ever really solve the problem."

If we want to resolve or prevent conflicts that happen when we prepare for outdoor activities, it helps to understand that the real problems may not be about the outdoor activity itself. Instead, they often reflect pent-up stresses from work, concerns about finances, parenting issues, personality conflicts between group members, or a host of other factors that would be present regardless of whether an outdoor activity is involved.

One way to appreciate this is to consider the kinds of thoughts that people might have but not express to one another during a pre-trip conflict. In the examples below, each person is really thinking two things. One thought is about the surface issue the conflict appears to be about. The accompanying, and usually unvoiced, thoughts in brackets are about the relationship.

"He knows I hate it when he pressures me like this." [All he cares about is getting to the river. He doesn't really care about me at all.]

"He knows I hate it when he doesn't get ready quickly." [Sometimes I think he doesn't want to do this at all. If he did, he'd get ready faster. I don't know why I even ask him to come along.]

"Easy for her to be in a hurry. I'm left to take care of the kids, the house, the dog, and everything else." [It's like that all the time, not just when we're going camping. This is just one more example.]

"If she would set some real expectations, the kids wouldn't be such slouches about getting ready." [This is just one more example of how she doesn't raise them like she should.]

"It's just darn inconsiderate. They are always late and the entire group always ends up waiting for them." [They're basically selfish people and I'm not sure why we keep inviting them.]

"It's no big deal; everybody's always a little late and I'm sure nobody minds." [Besides, they just set those early start times because they like to have everything under their control. They never ask us when we think we should get started.]

"Jeez. Our parents got mad at us because we forgot to bring extra socks." [Don't they realize we're just kids? It isn't any fun when they're always grumpy like that.]

"Honestly. Sometimes it seems like our kids haven't got any common sense at all. We have to tell them everything three times

before they finally understand and get it done." [Camping together isn't a break for us, it's just one more place to be parents under pressure.]

What must be understood is that arguing about the surface matters is unlikely to help us deal constructively with the underlying relationship issues. Unless we deal with the underlying issues, the surface conflicts and relationship accidents are likely to continue. This principle applies to conflicts during preparation as well as to conflicts that arise during or after an activity. How to deal with underlying conflicts once they are recognized is discussed later in chapter 10, Communication for Outdoor Partners.

CHAPTER 3

EXPERIENCE

"To begin with, they had a lot more experience than I did, and that made a big difference."

"When he said he loved to canoe, I thought that meant he went a lot. How was I to know he had only done it once and that was at a scout camp?"

SOMEONE ONCE SAID, "IN NATURE, EXPERIENCE IS THE BEST TEACHER. YOU just better hope it's someone else's experience." That statement originally had to do with preventing and dealing with outdoor emergencies, but it applies quite well to relationships. This chapter looks at the ways experience differences contribute to relationship accidents and how we can deal with such differences more constructively.

THE EFFECTS OF EXPERIENCE DIFFERENCES

Imagine two people who are planning to go backpacking. One has been backpacking for years, while her partner has only been on one or two day hikes and has never before spent a night outdoors. As you consider this couple, think of all the ways the differences in experience will affect each person and the outcome of their trip together.

The more experienced person is at home in the outdoors. She knows where to go, what to bring, what not to bring, how to use the equipment, and a host of other information acquired from previous outings. Having backpacked for years, she takes most of her knowledge and skill for granted and assumes everyone else has had similar experience. Intellectually, she knows that her partner hasn't packed before, but she has forgotten what it's like to go backpacking for the first time. As she thinks about the trip ahead, she focuses only on how much fun it will be and is unaware of the anxiety and insecurity her partner may be feeling.

In contrast, the inexperienced person may know very little. As a result, he will be dependent on his partner from beginning to end and is sure to make lots of mistakes. He will be in a strange environment and has only a minimal idea about what equipment is needed or how to use it. Not knowing what to expect in the outdoors, he may have a number of fears and questions but he is probably ashamed to express these lest he appear foolish. As he thinks about the trip ahead, he hopes it will be fun, but he is also concerned about all sorts of real and imagined dangers. Most of all, he is afraid he will embarrass himself and will disappoint his partner.

It may turn out that this couple will get along fine and will have a terrific time together. It may also be that a relationship accident is waiting to happen. Whenever there are differences in experience, a number of factors come into play that can cause conflicts. If those with less experience feel that an activity exceeds what they can manage, they are likely to feel overwhelmed, vulnerable, and frustrated. Conversely, if activities are consistently less demanding or exciting than more experienced partners enjoy, they are likely to feel unchallenged, bored, and, again, frustrated. Such feelings make it very difficult to have fun, and if you're not having fun it's hard to enjoy either the outdoors or the company of your partners.

One woman used the terms "overfunctioning" and "underfunctioning" to describe this pattern. Until she and her partner found a better way to communicate about their experiences and what they wanted to do together, their outdoor activities seemed to be filled with disappointment and conflict. "One of us was always pressed to 'overfunction' while the other was forced to 'underfunction,'" she said. "We never seemed to match it just right."

Another person described similar feelings in her relationship: "I was always feeling like I had to keep up and do better or I would let Russ down. He was stronger, had more experience, and just liked to do more challenging things than I enjoyed. I'd try to keep up just to make him happy, but no matter how hard I tried, I just couldn't do it the way he did, and I got tired of having to be someone I'm not."

EXPERIENCE REVIEWS

Identifying the problems that can stem from experience differences does not mean that everyone must be at the same experience level in order to get along. It does mean that differences must be carefully considered in the planning process and throughout the trip.

As a starting point to increase awareness and appreciation of experience levels, it is helpful for partners to review together what each person has done and knows about the planned activity. Some people may find this an awkward or intrusive process, but if it is explained that the purpose is to make sure everyone has fun and the plans match their interests and abilities, most folks don't have a problem.

When I review experience with people before an activity, I often start with an apology for having to ask about everyone's background in the activity. Then I explain that the issue is not to see if one person is "better" than another, it's just to be sure we all know what we're going to do so everyone can have a good time. The goal of this introduction is to allow everyone to feel comfortable enough to describe their experience as accurately and honestly as possible.

Experience reviews are particularly important for groups who have not done an activity together before. I have been on trips in which nothing was really said about experience until we arrived at the starting point, only to discover that one or two of the group were woefully unprepared. However awkward it might have been to ask detailed questions about experience before the trip, that certainly would have been preferable to discovering this after driving five hours to a river or trailhead.

Even for people who have done things together before, taking time to systematically review experience can help identify sources of conflict that may not have been understood previously. When a couple who had been backpacking together many times began to talk about what they knew how to do around camp, it emerged that one of the partners did not know how to set up the tent or start the stove on her own. As a result, she always felt dependent on her partner and was unable to help out as much as she wanted when they were camping.

For families, experience reviews are a good way to help parents remember to not take for granted what their children know. A father, who had been camping since he was a boy, was being unusually critical of his stepson for not knowing how to do any of the things the father assumed the boy should know. When it was pointed out that the boy had never really been camping before and had no way of knowing the things the father was upset about, he realized that instead of becoming frustrated he should be patient and take the time to help the boy learn.

As a guide to identify key experience differences, I have put together an experience checklist to help point out some of the experience differences most often cited as having contributed to conflicts. If the list sounds like it is asking you to be too precise or objective, there is a reason for the detail. Conflicts almost never arise because partners communicate "too clearly," but they often arise because partners do not communicate fully and accurately enough.

EXPERIENCE CHECKLIST

Instructions: Each person should answer the questions below as accurately and honestly as possible. Answer the questions for one activity at a time. If you are completing the checklist as a general review of your activities together, it is best to complete the exercise for one activity before considering another. If an activity involves several elements, complete the checklist separately for each of those elements. For example, if next week you are going for a weekend of cross-country skiing and winter camping, answer the questions once as they pertain to cross-country skiing, then complete the same checklist a second time for the winter camping element of your weekend. Each person in a family or group should complete the checklist individually, then the lists should be shared with one another.

Activity: _____

PART I: Experience and Skill Level

Answer each question as honestly as possible. Remember, it is far better to be accurate beforehand than for problems to emerge in the middle of an outing.

1. How many times have you have done this activity before in your life?_____

2. How would you rate your ability?
   A ___ Absolute beginner, no previous experience
   B ___ Novice
   C ___ Advanced novice
   D ___ Intermediate
   E ___ Advanced intermediate
   F ___ Expert
   G ___ Advanced expert

3. What is the average physical difficulty and skill level of your previous experiences? (If you can, try to answer this in terms of objective information, such as, "In the past two months, I have gone on weekly ten-mile hikes on flat ground," or "I go for fast fifteen-mile bike rides at least three times a week," or "I regularly climb class 5.8 rock," etc.)? _____

_____

4. What is the maximum physical difficulty and skill demands at which you have ever performed this activity? _____

_____

5. What is the level of difficulty and skill demand you most enjoy now?

_____

_____

PART II: Knowledge of Activity

6. How would you rate your overall knowledge of all aspects of the activity?

A ___ Absolute beginner, no previous experience

B ___ Novice

C ___ Advanced novice

D ___ Intermediate

E ___ Advanced intermediate

F ___ Expert

G ___ Advanced expert

7. How would you rate your knowledge of the equipment?

A ___ Know nothing about the equipment

B ___ Know the names of some equipment

C ___ Know the names, basic design of most equipment, and know how to use most of it

D ___ Have advanced knowledge of equipment design, features, and use of almost all equipment

8. How would you rate your knowledge of repairs and maintenance?

A ___ Know virtually nothing about repair or maintenance and have never performed any myself

B ___ Know simple repairs and maintenance and have performed them on a few occasions

C ___ Know moderately complex repairs and maintenance and have performed them on several occasions

D ___ Know virtually all repairs and maintenance and have performed them on multiple occasions

9. How would you rate your knowledge of risks and safety?

A ___ Know virtually nothing about risks and safety measures

B ___ Know something about risks and safety measures but have very little practical experience

C ___ Know quite a bit about risks and safety measures but have only limited practical experience

D ___ Have extensive knowledge of risks and experience using safety equipment

PART III: Importance of Experience, Skill, and Knowledge to You and the Others in Your Group

For the last part of the checklist, review the previous questions about experience, skill, and knowledge and ask yourself the following questions for each.

1. How important is it to you that you have a certain level of experience, skill, or knowledge yourself? Are you at the level you desire? If you were answering this question solely for yourself, without considering your partners' level of experience or desires, would your answer be any different? _____

   _____

2. How important is it to you that your partners have a certain level of experience, skill, or knowledge? Are your partners at the level you desire? _____

   _____

3. How important is it to your partners that they have a certain level of experience, knowledge, or skill? Are your partners at the level they desire? If your partners were deciding solely for themselves, without considering your level of experience or desires, would their answers be any different? _____

   _____

4. How important is it to your partners that you have a certain level of experience, knowledge, or skill? Are you at the level your partners desire? _____

   _____

WHAT THE CHECKLIST MEANS

The experience checklist really has two goals. The first is to help you assess, compare, and understand your own level of experience and that of your partners. The second goal is to help you assess what you and your partners feel about your respective levels of experience, skill, or knowledge.

The reason for these dual goals is that conflicts do not arise solely from differences in experience, nor do equal levels of experience or skill necessarily prevent conflict. Along with accurately appraising our levels of ability, we must also accurately appraise our expectations for ourselves and for our partners. Differences in experience and skill alone are less likely to produce conflicts than are differences between expectations or desires. People who are much different in experience and ability levels can get along just fine as long as it is okay with both of them that they are different and their plans take those differences into account. On the other hand, partners may be much more closely matched in experience or skill but if they have expectations that differ significantly, conflicts are likely to result.

KNOWING WHERE YOU ARE

If you have not thought and communicated clearly about your experience and what you enjoy doing, it is easy to be unrealistic with yourself about an activity or be cajoled by others into something that will not be enjoyable to you. Similarly, if your partners do not have clear ideas about their own experience, skills, or desires, you may influence them to do things they will not enjoy. This doesn't mean it's bad to adapt to one another or to occasionally be nudged beyond our level of comfort. But if we are unclear about our own desires and expectations, it's easy to blame or resent our partners when we feel uncomfortable about doing something.

Most of us probably know what happens then. We go along with the other person but only halfheartedly. As soon as things go less than perfectly, we begin thinking things like "this was their idea" or "I knew I shouldn't have come along; what a stupid thing to do." It may seem like the height of sharing or giving to do something just to please our partners, but if we are not up front about what we think or feel about doing something, what was meant as a positive gesture can easily turn negative later on.

The importance of knowing and expressing your own experience level and desires to your partners is demonstrated by the frequency with which the opening quote in this chapter—"to begin with, they had a lot more experience than I did, and that made a big difference"—was followed by something like "and to tell you the truth now, I really wasn't too sure about going in the first place." Countless relationship accident reports begin with these two statements. The lesson is that it is not just differences in experience that lead to trouble. It is also, and more importantly, the failure of everyone to communicate and understand what differences in experience and expectations mean to them and their partners.

With this in mind, when you discuss the Experience Checklist with your partners, set a ground rule that it is essential for each of you to say or ask whatever you really think or feel in response to the checklist or the planned activity. It is also essential to listen to and really hear what each person thinks and feels. Thus, if someone has always been afraid or uncomfortable about doing a certain activity, he or she needs to be able to say that—and to say it without fear that doing so will lead to ridicule or will somehow threaten the relationship. Similarly, if one person has always wanted the other to have a higher level of skill, she or he needs to be able to say that. Don't worry at this point about solving either of these problems or trying to answer questions the way your partners might want you to. The first step is to be honest about where each person is as a starting point.

COPING WITH EXPERIENCE DIFFERENCES IN COUPLES

One of the reasons couples are not open about differences in their experiences or expectations is a belief that differences threaten relationships. In reality, there are many creative ways of dealing with differences once both people are aware they exist.

The first point that should be understood is that just because two people form a couple does not mean they have to do everything together. Sometimes our fantasies of "the perfect partner" mean we will share everything with each other. That might be nice as fantasy, but for most couples it is simply unrealistic. People have different needs, abilities, and goals and there will be times when partners either do not want to do the same things or are not able to do them. Rather than bemoaning that fact, it is better to accept it and find ways to make it work. Three couples I interviewed had found their own ways of dealing with differences in experience and skill.

(1) Brad and Jennifer are both in their early thirties and have been together six years. They have a three-year-old son and just celebrated the birth of a baby girl. Although both parents have keen outdoor

interests and enjoy doing many things together, there are also things they do on their own or with other friends. For example, Brad enjoys mountaineering but Jennifer has no interest in the sport. It is fine for Jennifer that Brad enjoys climbing, but she feels no need to join him. She is very clear about this, and that, in turn, is fine with Brad.

The difference in interest has long since been managed successfully by this couple, but it sometimes surprises their friends. At a party where Brad and his climbing partners were showing slides of a recent climb, someone asked Jennifer if she was a climber too. "No," she said, "I find it all rather silly." Jennifer later told me that she had not said what she did as an insult to Brad or anyone else. She was merely expressing her opinion about climbing from her perspective. Far from being upset by this response, Brad appreciated her frankness. Jennifer's directness and honesty make it much easier for them to know when the other person really wants to do something and when he or she doesn't. Brad tries to afford Jennifer the same honesty and freedom to do things she enjoys without him. When I interviewed them, Jennifer had just returned from a two-week bicycle trip with her sisters. Brad had stayed home and cared for the baby during that time.

(2) Gerd and Marlis try to be together in some way in everything they do. To accomplish this, they purposefully find ways to compromise between their different skill levels or to involve each other in some way in their activities. I first met this couple on a trip down the Grand Canyon. Gerd, who was on the trip to celebrate his fiftieth birthday, made the trip in a kayak (without once tipping over). His wife Marlis went along with a commercial raft company. That arrangement allowed both to enjoy and share the experience, but they did not have to be at the same level of skill or strength as kayakers.

Traveling by kayak and raft was only one of the ways Gerd and Marlis managed to be together. They explained that when Gerd ran more technical rivers, Marlis went along to drive the shuttle car and provide other support before and after the kayaking. Over the years, Marlis also developed her own skills in a kayak so she could run certain rivers with Gerd. For his part, when he kayaked with Marlis, Gerd chose rivers they could do together that were less challenging than those he sometimes ran. They also owned a two-person kayak, which allowed them to paddle together on many rivers that Marlis might not have wanted to run on her own.

By one person enhancing her skill and the other adjusting to his partner's needs and abilities, Marlis and Gerd are able to enjoy their sport together. This approach has certainly worked for them, so well in fact that during our interview they had genuine difficulty identifying times when they did not get along or quarreled during more than twenty years of outdoor adventures together.

Gerd and Marlis chose their particular approach because for them the most important thing is being together. Their rationale is that, by making certain adjustments to be with the other, each person may not be having his or her own 100 percent ideal experience alone, but if as a couple each has an 80 percent positive experience, that adds up to a total of 160 percent. By comparison, if each person seeks the perfect experience for him or herself but disregards the other's needs, the result may be 100 percent positive for one person and 100 percent negative for the other. The net result is a total of 0 percent fun for the two as a couple. Still more typical, when there is no sensitivity or compromise, conflicts result that produce something closer to a 100 percent negative for both people.

(3) Laura and Dan both enjoy tennis, but Laura has played competitively since she was a child and regularly wins regional tournaments. Dan, on the other hand, took up the sport shortly before he and Laura met. They spoke of this difference in experience and skill in the following conversation:

> Dan: "I've always been very competitive at everything I do and for a long time I was determined to beat Laura at tennis. I took lessons, read books, and practiced as much as I could. But I could never beat her. It used to drive me nuts when I'd make my best serve and rush the net, and she'd pass or lob me like it was easy. The worst of all was when she aced me on her service. It wasn't tennis to me then, it was a personal insult."

> Laura: "I don't know how many fights we had about that. He'd challenge me to a match, I'd beat him, then he'd get angry. But if I let him win, I knew he'd just get even madder. The trouble was that no matter how much Dan practiced, he would never be able to make up for all the years of playing I had. Even when we practiced together, he was learning but I was still getting practice myself. He couldn't accept that I was better and it got to where I didn't want to play any more."

Dan then went on to explain how he was forced to acknowledge that there would always be differences in experience between himself and Laura and that Laura would always be a better tennis player. Because both were competitive, this was not easy, but they found it worked for them to focus their competitive impulses on matches with other people within their own ability rankings. By accepting their differences, and finding alternative ways of enjoying tennis and still being competitive, they were able to live with the fact that they could still be happy together even though one could best the other at a sport.

Clearly, there are many ways of managing experience and skill differences to bring positive results. The important thing is for each person to be honest about what she or he wants for her or himself, to respect and be sensitive to partners' needs and abilities, and to work together to find ways that satisfy both as individuals while still strengthening the relationship.

FAMILIES AND OUTDOOR EXPERIENCE
UNDERSTANDING THE EXPERIENCE OF CHILDREN

When people describe how it feels to be the least experienced member of a couple or group, they often say things like, "It feels like they're treating me like a child." That description speaks volumes about how experience differences affect adults, and how such differences produce lasting effects in children.

It would be wonderful if parents could occupy the minds and bodies of their children for just a few hours during an outdoor activity. The resulting insights might not alleviate all frustration or impatience that parents sometimes feel, but they would go a long way toward enhancing awareness of activities from the child's perspective.

Perhaps the closest we can come to being in the shoes of our own children is to recall what it was like when we first tried to learn a new activity from a parent or other adult. I can still remember the first time my father tried to teach me to fly-fish. My father is an avid fly-fisherman who can almost caress the line across a river. To speak of fly-fishing as an "activity" is tantamount to sacrilege. For my father, fly-fishing is religion of the highest order. It is ritual, prayer, and direct physical communion with the deity. Best of all, it is free of dogma. Fish can neither read nor quote scripture and their habits are controlled by mysterious forces that neither stone tablets nor hatch guides will ever fully contain.

It might seem there could be no better way to learn to fly-fish than from my father. Nevertheless, I can still remember what happened when, after an hour or so of instruction, he let me try my luck on my own. As every back cast snarled the line in trees, and more than a few forward casts left a fishhook embedded somewhere in my clothing or body, my eyes began to well with tears. It wasn't from the pain of the hooks. It was from the feeling of utter frustration as I found myself completely incapable of doing something that my father made so easily beautiful and I wanted desperately to share with him.

Fortunately, Dad came back to check on me, saw the tears, and helped me untangle the line from branches that were beyond my reach. Then we walked to the stream bank and he took out a chocolate bar he'd been saving for lunch. After the snack and some stories about his first time fly-fishing, Dad asked if he could borrow my rod for a moment. We went back to the stream and with a flick of his wrist he put the fly right into a calm pool near shore. Then he handed me the rod, stood quietly behind me, and within seconds I was struggling to play the first trout I ever landed with a fly rod. It turned out that Dad had been watching the fish in that pool since we first reached the river, but he had waited all morning just to watch me catch it.

Looking back, what stands out most for me now is how hurt I felt when I couldn't do something and how important it was that my father understood my pain and found a way to turn it into a success. He could have yelled at me for tangling the line, or criticized my casting, or said we should just go home. But instead he told me it was okay, I was okay, and then we caught a fish together. That was his way and I will always be grateful for it.

As parents think about outdoor activities with their family, they would do well to imagine what the experience is like from the perspective of each different family member. How does the youngest one feel if everyone can do the activity better than he or she can? Or, if the situation is reversed, what must an older sibling feel if she or he always has to teach the littler ones or if a younger brother or sister surpasses her or him?

The parents of two children, ages six and eight, told me how upon arrival at a sledding hill they discovered that the youngest child had worn his regular school shoes instead of boots. "I'm kind of ashamed to admit it," the father said, "but my first response was to yell at Jeremy for being so foolish. Then my eight-year-old reminded me that

Jeremy had never been sledding before so he didn't know what to do. It was actually my fault for assuming that a six-year-old boy should know everything there is to know about sledding. I guess it's lucky for me nobody yells at me for not knowing everything there is to know about parenting."

ADAPTING ACTIVITIES TO CHILDREN

Parents who successfully involve children in outdoor activities think carefully about activities from the children's perspective. They adapt their activities to meet the needs of different family members and they gradually build the children's level of experience and comfort. The length of outings, physical demands, weather conditions, and other factors are all taken into account and adjustments are made as needed so the children can learn and have fun. With adaptations to meet the needs of children, parents often discover that children who might say they don't like an activity really mean they don't like it under certain conditions. As conditions are changed to better meet their needs, the same children will often have much more fun and want to go again.

Chris and Pat are parents of a seven-year-old girl who loves to go hiking and backpacking. Their daughter's enjoyment of the outdoors did not come about by accident. It was the result of a caring and well thought-out process. Chris and Pat described the start of that process with a lovely story:

> Pat: "We wanted Katherine to be comfortable with nature from the very start. As soon as we could, we went for short trips with her in a baby backpack, and before she could even walk we let her play and crawl around in mountain meadows."
>
> Chris: "All along we tried to be sure her experiences were positive. Sometimes we worried too much about this at first, but we found out that she really didn't seem to mind some things we thought might bother her."
>
> Pat: "I remember the first time it rained while we were out with her. She was maybe six or seven months old. When the first drops landed on her, she made kind of a sour face, looked at us, and acted like she might cry. Then Chris smiled back at her and softly said it was raining and wasn't it wonderful. Katherine smiled back and kind of laughed."

Chris: "It might sound weird, but I tried at that moment to think about how magic the rain is and how life depends on it. And I tried to communicate that awareness to Katherine and I think somehow she got it. It's amazing what kids can pick up."

Pat: "What was so great about it was that if Chris had acted like rain was something bad, Katherine probably would have learned that. But instead she knows how neat rain is."

From that beginning, Chris and Pat introduced their daughter to short hikes, then overnight trips. For each activity, they carefully try to match the activity's demands with the ability and readiness of Katherine. This doesn't mean every trip is without difficulty, but it does reduce the number and severity of the problems, and most of the time things go very well.

Each family must find their own way to accommodate individual differences. Your approach may not be the same as another family's, but you may want to review your activities to see how you are taking developmental factors, experience, skill, and other differences into account as you select the things you will do as a family.

USING RESOURCES BEYOND THE FAMILY

It can also be helpful to make use of resources outside the family. For example, most ski areas have special lessons for children as young as four or five, and many areas now offer day care for younger children. Outdoor clubs and organizations often have activities designed for people of different ages and abilities. Even organized bicycle racing has divisions in which children who are just barely off their training wheels can do one-lap criteriums. By taking advantage of such opportunities, parents reduce the burden of constantly supervising children on their own. At the same time, participating in activities with people other than their parents can help children develop valuable social skills and friendships.

Involving children in lessons or group activities can be a beneficial experience for the children and offers a needed break for parents, but it is still important for parents to spend time doing the activities together with the children. Thus, parents at a ski slope may want to make some runs with their kids before or after the ski classes. Parents should remember, however, that if their children have just spent an hour or so in instruction, the parents do not have to continue the class after the instructor leaves. Instead, they can just have fun with their children and compliment them for what they have learned and the progress they are making.

The key to all of this is to accept that children are children and are not just miniature adults. If children are introduced gradually to outdoor activities, and if activities are selected to match their experience and interests, the foundation will be in place for years of enjoyable family outings. On the other hand, if early outdoor experiences are negative, children and parents alike may well decide that it is easier to just stay inside and watch TV.

EXPERIENCE DIFFERENCES IN GROUPS

The best ways to deal with experience differences among groups of people depends on the nature of the groups. Informal groups of friends do not face the same challenges as formal organizations, but the issue must be addressed successfully whatever the nature of the partnerships involved.

One of the ways groups can deal with differences in experience is by providing a variety of different activities designed to meet different types of needs and experience levels. Established outdoor groups typically offer outings ranging from absolute beginner to expert levels. Members then choose which activities are commensurate with their levels of experience and desires.

Groups of friends may not be able to simultaneously provide options for different levels of activities, but they can make a purposeful effort to vary the level of difficulty over time so those not up to more demanding activities, and perhaps less gung ho partners, can participate on occasion.

Along with offering activities at different levels, most organized groups have learned that it is essential to clearly specify the level of experience or difficulty for each trip. Simply announcing "there will be a hike on Saturday" or "there will be a sea kayaking trip on Sunday" is an almost sure ticket to disaster. It is far better to have some form of standard rating or ranking system that communicates the experience and skill required. An example of one such ranking system is that used by The Mountaineers, an organization of more than 15,000 members in Washington State. In every issue of their monthly newsletter, the opening of their listing of hikes begins with the following information:

Trip Classifications (may change due to trail conditions):
(E)   Easy: Up to 8 miles round trip, up to 1,200 feet elevation gain
(M)   Moderate: Up to 12 miles, 1,200–2,500 feet elevation gain
(S)   Strenuous: Up to 14 miles, 2,500–3,500 feet elevation gain
(VS)   Very Strenuous: Over 14 miles and/or more than 3,500 feet
           elevation gain

This rating system is followed by a list of required equipment, information about sign-up and cancellation procedures, and where to call for any questions. Particularly noteworthy is the policy statement within the equipment section: *"It is Mountaineers policy that leaders leave inadequately clothed or shod hikers, or unprepared hikers, at the trailhead."*

Years of experience and thousands of outings have taught this group that it is essential to be as clear as possible about requirements and expectations. Every hike or other outing listed contains information about difficulty, experience, equipment, and other pertinent information. Members are then free to choose those activities that best suit them. If members choose something for which they are unprepared, the policy reserves the leader's discretion in deciding whether they should come along.

Established organizations such as The Mountaineers have some advantages over informal groups of friends. Because of the organization's size, structure, and policies, if a leader determines that someone is not sufficiently prepared for the trip, the decision—though it may not be welcomed by an individual who is excluded—is less likely to be taken as a personal affront that spoils a friendship. In less formal groups, which typically do not have an established ranking system, formal policy, or clearly identified leaders, exclusion of someone from an activity may be taken as personal rejection. This situation can place friends and informal leaders in very uncomfortable positions.

One way to deal with experience differences among friends is to use the experience checklist presented earlier in this chapter. If each person completes the checklist, it is not left solely to friends or an informal leader to tell a member he or she is not sufficiently experienced for an activity. That fact can be demonstrated by comparing the person's experience level with others who will be along.

Still, sometimes it happens that people deceive themselves and one another when talking about their experience. Nature, however, will not be deceived. Whether one is in an organized club or a less formal group of friends, if risks are involved, each person must be responsible for accurately appraising his or her own skills and the skills of others. If someone is not up to a task for whatever reason, that simply must be addressed. Friends do not do friends any favors by letting them come on activities for which they are not qualified. However difficult it may be, someone in a group may have to decide that another member should not come along. Once again, it is better to make this decision before a trip is underway.

If it falls to you to speak to someone who you don't think should participate in a trip, try to consider how that person is feeling and to talk about those feelings as well as your own. For example, you might say, "Richard, this is really hard for me but I think this trip is too difficult for you. I know how much you want to come along, and I'd love to have you, but I think you're just not ready for it yet." Most of the time, if you show sensitivity and demonstrate that you're sincerely concerned, people will appreciate your position and accept your judgment.

On rare occasions, it may be necessary to be still more assertive. I once had to tell someone, "Look. I know you want to come, but you have to understand this can kill you. It isn't just a matter of thinking you can or wanting to be able to. You have to know without a doubt that you have the skills, because if you don't, you or someone else might die. You aren't at that level yet and I won't do this with you." Such blunt statements are rarely needed, but if the alternative is to allow someone to endanger him or herself or others, tough decisions must be made. More is said about this topic in chapter 4, Physical Preparation.

BUILDING EXPERIENCE TOGETHER

Along with considering each person's individual experience in a challenging or extended activity, it is also important to realistically consider how much experience each person has doing things with the intended partners. Often people who have done relatively little together set out on major adventures, then are surprised to discover they do not get along as well as they thought they would.

The principle of gradually building experience together applies equally to couples, families, and groups. For example, it would probably not be a good idea for a family's first outing to be a six-day raft trip down a wilderness river. Similarly, a couple who has never been camping before would be ill advised to plan a two-week African safari as a honeymoon. This advice may seem obvious, but people make these kinds of mistakes all the time, then wonder what happened when the relationship falls apart. The key is to pay at least as much attention to the relationship as you do to all the other aspects of an activity. If experience is indeed the best teacher, it is far more pleasant to learn from positive experiences rather than negative ones.

One woman related how she and a friend with whom she had carpooled to work decided to go on a three-month trip to eastern Europe. This decision was reached without considering the fact that, apart from their drives to work, they had done little else together. In fact, they had never before spent more than a full day in each other's company.

It turned out that the two had completely different styles and expectations for traveling. After just two weeks, they were almost at each other's throats. Unable to continue together, they parted ways somewhere in Hungary and did not get back together until several months after both had returned to the United States.

A potentially more dangerous experience was related by a man who set out to climb a 20,000-foot South American peak with two people he had met a month earlier at a health club but with whom he had never even gone on so much as a day hike. The relationship did not work out and the team broke up while still on the mountain. The man was able to get down safely on his own, but if there had been an accident or serious illness, the consequences of the relationship failure could have been grave.

The lesson from such reports is clear. The success of outdoor adventures often depends on the success of relationships. And the success of outdoor relationships does not depend solely on people sharing similar levels of interest or experience in an activity. Relationship success often depends more on prior experience doing similar activities together. Therefore, before undertaking any extended or difficult trips or activities, partners are well advised to start with small activities together and build from there. Day hikes, overnighters, and multiday journeys of gradually increasing difficulty are a prudent sequence. If the relationship still holds after meeting more demanding situations, partners will know they can get along and will have established a base for future challenges.

CHAPTER 4

PHYSICAL PREPARATION

"When she said it would be an easy hike,
I had no idea that easy for her meant five hours of uphill climb."

"If we had known our friends were so out of shape,
we probably never should have invited them."

SHORTLY AFTER HE MOVED FROM CONNECTICUT TO COLORADO, a friend of mine read in the paper about a day hike to see alpine wildflowers. He eagerly signed up and arrived at the appointed departure site, but he was rather disappointed to discover that his fellow hikers were all in their late fifties or older. "Oh well," he thought, "this won't be much of a challenge, but at least I'll learn some things about flowers." As it turned out, by the end of the day he had learned about more than flowers.

My friend started the hike at a pace that might have worked at sea level but was much too fast for the mile-high air of Colorado. It wasn't long before he began to feel sick and dizzy and was forced to slow. Much to his chagrin, he was soon passed by the rest of the group and found himself bringing up the rear of the party. Were it not for the frequent stops to admire flowers, and for the kindness and patience of a woman who he later learned was in her early seventies, my friend would have been left far behind. Describing the experience several days later, he confessed, "Basically, those folks walked me flat into the dirt. Pretty humbling, I gotta tell you."

Apart from a slightly bruised ego, my friend's experience produced no lasting damage and provided valuable lessons about both hiking at altitude and stereotypes. It also demonstrated the role of physical conditioning in outdoor activities.

Differences in physical abilities contribute to countless relationship accidents. When our physical abilities are overtaxed, we spend so much effort just to meet the physical demands that we easily become upset with our partners. As we fight to cope with exhaustion or pain, it becomes more difficult to appreciate and enjoy the natural surroundings. All these things could be prevented or at least substantially reduced if partners were more aware of their own capacities and the physical demands of activities.

DEALING WITH PHYSICAL DEMANDS OF OUTDOOR ACTIVITIES
PHYSICAL PREPARATION CHECKLIST

To deal effectively with physical elements of outdoor activities, the following points should be kept in mind.

- Start small and build up gradually. Select initial activities so people can complete them with plenty of strength and energy to spare.
- Plan outings that are within the physical capacity of the participants, as demonstrated by what the participants have done previously.
- Be sure everyone understands the physical demands of the planned

activity. Offer explicit, detailed descriptions of the plans, compare the planned activity with activities each person has previously performed, and request objective information about each person's level of fitness.

- Emphasize the importance of being honest and make it safe for people to express concerns about their own physical condition or that of others.
- Train sufficiently to complete the planned activity with some degree of physical reserves left.
- Do some preparatory physical activities together with partners so each person is aware of one another's conditioning.
- If an activity will test limits, be sure each person is familiar with the experience of pushing personal limits in some similar way and is prepared for that experience on this occasion.
- If illness, injury, or lack of training might impede a person's ability to participate as planned, then either the plans should be changed or that person should bow out of the activity.
- Provide decision points during an outing so that people can evaluate their fitness and choose to go on or select another option.
- When planning outdoor activities with families, keep in mind that it is always easier to adapt the physical activity to the family than the family to the activity.
- If individuals do not make realistic decisions about their own physical capacities, group leaders or others may have to use their best judgment and act accordingly. This might mean changing group plans, informing the fittest members that a planned activity may be slower than they are used to, or telling those who are not fit enough that they should not be part of a particular trip.

STARTING SMALL AND BUILDING UP

If you want to squelch people's enthusiasm for the outdoors, a good way to do so is to start them out at levels beyond their physical abilities. On the other hand, if you want to get partners off to a good start, choose immediate goals they are sure to reach. The ideal first experience is one in which people feel challenged but successful. Your partners should come home with a sense that they have pushed themselves a bit but are ready for more.

This principle applies to all outdoor activities. If someone is going on a first hike, choose a trail that is long on beauty and short on distance. If you're planning a canoe trip with beginners, pick a destination just far enough away to give a sense of adventure, but close enough to keep the muscle aches and blisters to a minimum.

An experienced scout leader said it very well: "With beginners, the thing to do is focus on how folks feel at the end, not where they went. The goal isn't really to get to a place. It's to get people to have fun. If you can do that, the trip was a success wherever you ended up on a map."

Another group leader suggested that a good way to think about starting small is to abandon the concept of a destination entirely. "Instead of planning to hike to a specific place, I like to think in terms of time. When I go with beginners I tell them how long we'll be out, not how far or where we'll go. Then I pick an easy trail, start out at a leisurely pace, and see how everyone is doing. If people are going pretty well, we may get a little further up the trail. If they are a little slower, we take plenty of rest stops and don't get so far. Either way we always start back a little before our time is half up. This keeps the focus on enjoying nature and having fun together rather than going fast or far."

STAYING WITHIN PEOPLE'S PHYSICAL LIMITS

Staying within people's limits makes sense, but it is not always easy for the very experienced or highly fit to tone down their activities for their partners' benefit. A woman marathoner explained her experience of running with her husband: "My regular runs are usually eight or ten miles a day with longer runs on weekends. My husband is only to the point where he can run three miles and that's at a pretty slow pace. Sometimes he wants me to run with him, but it's really hard for me to go for such short distances and so slowly. To me, it doesn't feel like I'm running at all."

This woman was not belittling her husband's abilities. In fact, she was glad that he was training and she did everything she could to support him. Nevertheless, it was difficult for her to stay at his pace and distance limitations without getting frustrated. The solution they arrived at was to agree that on most days they would run separately, but once or twice a week she would start her regular runs early, then join her husband and run at his pace as a form of "cool down" for her.

A different approach was described by a man who found that when he went backpacking with his family, he had to dramatically change his thinking about the kinds of destinations and trails he chose.

"The worst thing I could do with the kids was to get stuck on reaching some place that required a long or steep hike. When I'm on my own or with a friend, we can easily go ten or fifteen miles a day. With the kids, a mile or two is probably the best distance. That used to drive me nuts, but now I take along books about plants or birds and I have learned to enjoy going slower and taking more in. It's not the physical challenge I'm used to, but there are other rewards and it's a lot more fun for me if the family is having a good time."

Each of these people had to adapt their usual level of physical demands to meet the needs of their partners. Doing so took some creativity and required them to be flexible, but the results, i.e., satisfied partners, were worth the changes. They could have insisted that everyone perform to their maximum levels and push the limits each time they went out, but the results would almost certainly have been negative.

ASSESSING PHYSICAL ABILITIES AND ACTIVITY DEMANDS

Evaluating levels of fitness and assessing how demanding an activity will be is not easy because no one can know exactly what someone else can accomplish, and it is hard to gauge the demands of something unless one has done it before.

For example, a description of a climbing route might read: "From base camp at 10,000 feet to the summit at 14,410 feet, requires between six to eight hours of climbing. Most climbers begin at 1:00 or 2:00 A.M. to reduce the risk of ice- and rockfall. In addition to climbing hardware, i.e., ropes, ice axe, crampons, etc., climbers should carry extra clothing, food, and sufficient equipment for emergency bivouacs."

It takes just a few seconds to read these short sentences, but really knowing what it means to spend eight hours climbing above 10,000 feet is something else entirely. Unless one has previously done something similar, there is no mental model or memory to draw from to imagine what will be required. Given the sedentary lives that most of us now live, it is really rather remarkable that people can actually do the kinds of climbs described above. Even those who exercise regularly probably get in less than one or two hours of sustained workout a day. Yet now they will be trying to go for eight hours at altitude— and that, remember, is just to get to the top.

Similar issues could arise for a host of other activities. What does it take physically to bicycle 20 miles, or 50 miles, or 100 miles? If a person runs 5 to 10 miles a day, does that mean he or she will be fit to make a 3-mile crossing against tides and wind in a sea kayak? There is a critical difference between simply talking about plans for an activity and really having an awareness of what the activity involves and whether everyone is up to it.

One way to address this problem is to provide more useful and easily interpreted information about the planned activity. Instead of offering brief route descriptions and asking if people think they want to go, more detailed descriptions can be presented that include accurate and explicit facts about conditions and physical demands. This can be made even more effective if otherwise abstract numbers are put into some framework people can more easily relate to. For example, rather than saying simply that a climb involves a vertical gain of 4,000 feet, one might add, "So, in other words, if you figure that it takes at least two or three steps for each foot of elevation gained, that is going to mean something like doing 10,000 or so knee bends with thirty or so extra pounds on your back for each bend and significantly less available oxygen than you are used to, and all this will have to be done in cold temperatures and after very little sleep."

Such descriptions can enhance awareness and improve estimates of demands and abilities. This helps novices appreciate what the activity may require. It can also help experienced partners more accurately gauge whether they can realistically expect others to be up to the task. Still, however, the decision depends to a large degree on each person making her or his own judgments about personal fitness in relation to the activity.

BEING HONEST ABOUT ABILITIES AND CONCERNS

Regardless of how accurately information is conveyed about the physical requirements of an activity, often people are aware of their physical condition and recognize that the demands exceed their limits, but they do not say anything for fear of upsetting their partner. Each person in the relationship contributes to this situation. The one who is not expressing his or her concerns is failing to communicate important information, but this is often because a partner has not been receptive or supportive in the past.

It is a fine thing to ask, "How does this sound to you?" but too often the unspoken message beneath the question is, "You'd better say it's fine because if you don't I will doubt your abilities and maybe even question if we should do anything at all together." This is a no-win situation because partners who feel an activity is beyond their capacity can either acquiesce to go along, knowing they will be unpleasant if they do, or decline, knowing their partner will be disappointed. In these circumstances, partners need to talk first about how they communicate and what their communications mean. Then they can begin to talk about the activity itself.

PHYSICAL TRAINING AND PREPARATION TOGETHER

On the most traveled climbing route of Mount Hood, the final pitch to the summit is a rather steep and narrow chute of snow and ice. Because so many people climb the route, "traffic jams" are common and it is possible to be stuck waiting for as much as an hour or more to go up the chute. During one early spring climb, as we waited below an extremely slow group above, I looked up uneasily at the sun and became concerned about the danger of ice- or rockfalls.

Eventually, I grew tired of waiting below the other parties and began chopping my own steps to make a parallel route for our group. As we passed other climbers, I could hear that some were breathing quite heavily and they seemed to be moving only a step or so a minute. After we reached the summit and parties we had passed began to arrive, I asked a young man who seemed to have been going the slowest how he had prepared for the climb. His answer was astonishing: "Not at all," he said rather proudly. "Some friends asked if I wanted to come along and I said sure. They told me it would be easy." Trying to contain my frustration, I pursued the questioning. "Do you run, or bike, or do anything?" "Well," he replied, "I did do a little walking this past week to get ready, but other than that, nothing. Pretty neat that I made it, huh?"

Judging from his comments, this person appeared completely unaware that his lack of preparation inconvenienced the rest of his party and all of the other climbers on the route. Beyond inconvenience, he also put himself and others at significantly increased risk.

The problem this example illustrates is unfortunately quite common. People who have little or no experience in the outdoors tend to not realize that the rules of the game are different. In the city, if you get tired of walking you can catch a cab, call a friend, or find some other way to deal with the situation. Similarly, in sports such as running, the worst that is likely to happen is you might get sick to your stomach or have to walk. Physical exhaustion in a wilderness setting can be far more consequential. On a mountain or in other comparable settings, one simply cannot not go on.

Because both the physical demands and the consequences are greater in the outdoors, planning to do an activity with others should involve a commitment to prepare physically. Even with sufficient preparation, it sometimes happens that unexpected events, such as illness or injury, limit one's abilities. Most partners accept that this can happen to anyone and they are willing to work around it without conflict. As long as each person trained and did his or her best to prepare, experienced partners are likely to say, "Hey, this can happen to anybody, it could happen to me too. We'll just have to change our plans this time."

On the other hand, if people who have not worked to prepare themselves sufficiently give out in the middle of a trip, their partners are likely to be justifiably upset. The choice should be to do what is necessary to prepare or be honest and direct with partners that one is not up to the activity. As with many other aspects of outdoor relationships, it may not be easy to tell partners we cannot join them because we are not sufficiently fit, but it is much better to deal with this before the trip starts than to be forced to acknowledge it in the middle when everyone may have to turn back.

In most cases, the issue of physical preparation is left up to each person to deal with individually. Often, there is no explicit discussion of the subject at all before starting the activity. This is usually a mistake. Unless one is very familiar with one's partners and has done similar activities together before, it is very important to talk directly and in detail about how each person has prepared.

Beyond merely talking about conditioning, it is a good idea to actually do some physical activities together on a preparation trip with one's partners. This serves several purposes. First, it builds group cohesion and helps people get to know each other. Second, it can be part of the physical training process. Third, if some members are not in condition for the final trip, this can be discovered by how they cope with the preparation trips. Excessive fatigue during a preparation trip provides objective evidence that allows people to decide they should either increase their training or not go on the more demanding activity.

EXPERIENCE IN PUSHING PHYSICAL LIMITS

When a planned activity is beyond people's normal limits, it is not always possible or advisable for preparation trips to be of the same duration or intensity. For example, if people are in training for an extended backpack trip or a particularly high mountain climb, it is hard to match the demands of the activity itself during the training process. It is, however, important for people to know they will be pushing their physical limits when they go on the final activity. It is also important for everyone to have some experience of going beyond their normal limits so they know what this feels like both physically and emotionally.

An experienced climber told how he was able to manage climbs much more successfully than people who were actually in "better shape" than he was when it came to training runs or bicycle trips. In fact, he trained quite hard and was by most standards in excellent condition, but his point was that something more than just physical fitness was the key to his success.

"I think a big part of it is that I have learned over time how to pace myself so I don't overdo it. I keep a slow and steady pace so I don't get burned out early and I always have some reserve. I really listen to my body and adjust accordingly. The other thing that makes a difference is that I have probably learned how to deal with feeling awful without feeling awful. What I mean is that by now I have done so many climbs that I know what it feels like to have to work to breathe and to want to stop or to ache all over. When someone feels like this for the first time, they think, 'Oh my god, I'm dying, I can't go on.' But after a while you get used to it and say, 'Yep, here it is again, my old friend pain.' That gives you a completely different attitude. You know it hurts and you know even before you go that it's going to hurt and that is just part of the price you're going to pay. But you also find ways of dealing with it and you know that the reward is worth the price."

Comparable ideas were voiced by a woman who goes on very long solo canoe trips: "I call it 'running on reserve tanks.' It's not something you can do all the time, but sometimes on these long trips, things come up and you just have to draw on your reserves to get you through. There is that point when you go beyond what's comfortable, then you go still farther beyond what's painful, then you go still farther because you don't have a choice. I don't especially like being in that space, but I know I can handle it if it comes up and that's very important."

In preparing for activities that may require people to push themselves exceptionally hard, each person should know what that experience is like and how they handle it. Coping well with such physical demands is especially important to avoiding relationship conflicts because it is all too easy when things get hard to start looking for someone to blame for our discomfort. If we know that fatigue and pain are sometimes just part of the game, we are less likely to try and find fault or get angry with our partners. Instead of getting angry at one another, partners can acknowledge that everyone is suffering and that shared experience can actually deepen the connection and commitment. These are also times when a sense of humor can help lighten the mood and help everyone keep going.

PLANNING FOR OPTIONS ALONG THE WAY

No matter how well people have prepared for an activity and understand its demands, it is always a good idea to include and discuss some form of contingency plans as part of the preparation process. For example, the primary plan for a backpacking trip might be to hike to a certain lake or meadow on the first day of a trip, but a shorter alternative could also be identified in case it turns out that people find themselves slower or more tired than they had anticipated. This is by no means an uncommon occurrence. Even experienced hikers sometimes overestimate their abilities or underestimate the weight of their packs and the effects of elevation gains and trail conditions.

By including options as part of the planning process, people feel safe to talk about how they are doing along the way. Rather than feeling they are somehow "spoiling" the trip if they become tired, they can instead suggest that for them it would be better to use the optional plan that everyone agreed upon as a possibility before starting out.

I remember a trip in which we all started out feeling very strong and with optimistic goals of reaching a lake that was seventeen miles from the trailhead. In the first few miles, we were even talking about some short climbs we might do in the afternoon after we reached the lake. All easily said at two miles in, but at fifteen miles, after a 2,000-foot elevation gain in the last two miles, everyone was quite ready to call it a day and save the lake for tomorrow. This decision was made easier because we had talked before about where we might camp if it turned out that we were tired or did not reach the lake as we had hoped.

Including options in planning is also wise from a safety perspective. In addition to providing a known place to rest or take shelter in the event of unexpected conditions, identifying where this might happen can help guide searchers in the case of emergencies. When route descriptions are left with friends or family members who will not be along, it's a good practice to indicate primary plans as well as any alternatives that might be taken.

FAMILIES

If there is one principle of outdoor relationships that would save the most conflicts in families it is this: *It is always easier to adapt the activity to the family than the family to the activity.*

When it comes to physical aspects of outdoor activities, it is essential to be realistic and conservative about the expectations one has for what family members can and cannot do. Wanting a spouse or children to be able to do something does not make them able to do it, and becoming angry or frustrated does not increase anyone's capacity, but it will surely decrease their enjoyment. Rather than setting goals that are too demanding and expecting family members to achieve them, it is far better to select goals that are within reach so everyone can have a good time and feel a sense of togetherness and accomplishment.

Many of the suggestions for how partners can deal with physical demands are equally applicable to families. It can be more difficult, but at the same time even more important, for adults to accurately gauge and communicate about the physical abilities of children. Adults are also likely to underestimate how quickly physical discomfort can change the emotional state of children.

STARTING SMALL

A woman who hiked for years before having children told me that when she first started taking her children for backpack trips, the word "tiny" kept coming to mind and helped her keep things in perspective.

"I realized how small the children are compared to us. Their legs are shorter, their hands are smaller; everything about them seemed so 'tiny' to me. That image made me realize that I would have to think small about the things we do. They could only carry small packs, and we would have to go shorter distances and for shorter times. We also take more breaks along the way and I try to avoid extreme weather conditions. This keeps the kids happy, and if they are happy it sure makes my job easier."

This woman's approach to keeping the physical elements within children's abilities is also consistent with the principle of starting small and building up gradually. Like people who are first starting outdoor activities, children may feel more vulnerable and the line between fun and misery is likely to be fine. If children become exhausted or hurt on early outings, their memories of those experiences are likely to be unpleasant and they are less likely to want to go again.

One man I spoke with described how he feared he may have spoiled his stepson's enjoyment of the outdoors by taking him on trips that were too demanding for the early stage of their relationship and for the boy's experience in the outdoors.

"I really wanted to teach him about the outdoors and to get to know him, so I planned a really neat three-day camping and fishing trip," the stepfather told me. "I thought it would be great, but it didn't work out at all. The hike was too far for him and he wasn't used to carrying a pack. Then it got cold at night, and the next day the mosquitoes were really bad. He was a pretty good sport about it all, but the next time I asked if he wanted to go he said no thanks, he really didn't think he liked backpacking. Instead he stayed home and played video games all weekend."

PHYSICAL TRAINING

Some children are naturally drawn to athletic or outdoor activities and it is easy for them to stay in shape and be ready for whatever comes up. Others prefer more sedentary pursuits and are unlikely to be in condition for demanding activities. While one might be able to encourage adults to train and prepare to go on a special trip, expecting a similar response from children is probably unrealistic.

No matter how much parents might want to share a special outdoor experience with children, if the children are not up to the task physically, the parents may just have to accept that fact. Often, as they mature, children decide on their own that they want to be able to do more things and staying fit is part of that process. If parents are patient, they may eventually be able to enjoy activities they have wanted to share with their kids, but it may take a few more years to reach that point.

RESOURCES

For families who enjoy the outdoors with children, an outstanding resource is the "Best Hikes With Children™" series of books published by The Mountaineers. These are available for a number of states, including Oregon, Washington, Colorado, the New England area, and others. In addition to providing valuable tips for keeping kids happy along the trail, these books present usable descriptions of "kid-tested" trails.

If guidebooks are not available for your area, other good resources may include local outdoor or hiking groups. Sierra Club, Audubon, and other such organizations often have members who hike with their families and children and would be happy to recommend destinations. Scouting organizations, including Boy Scouts, Girl Scouts, and Campfire, may also have some suggestions.

GROUPS

Physical abilities and differences pose special challenges for outdoor organizations or groups of friends. Among the most common problems in groups are a lack of information about each person's physical abilities, keeping people of different abilities together once trips are underway, and dealing with situations in which members are not sufficiently prepared for a given activity.

PHYSICAL DIFFERENCES IN GROUPS

The wider the disparity between the most and least fit members of a group, the greater the potential for problems. The trouble is that assessing physical abilities of group members is not easy. Even good friends may not be aware of one another's physical condition, and it is not possible to know the physical abilities of every member of an outdoor organization.

In many outdoor organizations, people who have never met before come together for the first time on hikes or climbs. The question of physical preparation may be talked about in general terms, but the decision about who is or is not fit enough is usually left to each individual to determine. Members may have doubts about their own capacity or that of others, but social pressures and needs for self-esteem make it difficult for people to be fully honest about their own abilities or their concerns about others.

As a result, most groups tend to deal with physical differences by not dealing with them. In the most common scenario, everyone who shows up is allowed to start together. Once a trip is underway, those who are exceptionally fit relative to the rest of the group are less likely to experience exhaustion, pain, or other discomforts that others may encounter. They may, however, find themselves frustrated at the slower pace or frequent breaks of their companions. On the other hand, those who are less fit and are pushed beyond their comfort level or normal abilities may resent the stronger members and resist pressures to go faster. This is when relationship problems emerge. It is also when dangerous decisions are sometimes made.

KEEPING GROUPS TOGETHER

If differences in physical abilities lead group members to become separated, or if relationship conflicts cause people to become angry with one another and break apart, the emotional and physical cohesion of a group is lost. Stories of accidents following such separations are numerous and sometimes tragic.

An example of how easily this can happen was described by a teacher who led a group of students on a sea kayaking trip in Baja California, Mexico. While kayaking in the waters of Magdalena Bay, some of the stronger students were soon far ahead of the rest of their party. Unfortunately, the lead paddlers were stronger physically but they were no more experienced than the other students. As they charged ahead on what seemed to be glassy, calm water, a strong tidal current was rapidly carrying them toward the mouth of the bay and the surf of the open ocean. Realizing the danger, the teacher had to leave the slower students and paddle for all he was worth to catch the group ahead. Fortunately, he arrived in time and turned the students upstream to ferry against the now-quickening tidal flow. After several minutes of very hard going, everyone managed to reach the shore just about fifty yards before the surf line.

That experience demonstrated the importance of everyone in the group staying within easy communication range at all times. In this situation, the group was fortunate that nothing serious happened, but there are similar stories of deaths that occurred because people became separated on kayaking trips, climbs, and even day hikes. To prevent such tragedies, before the group begins a trip, they must discuss the importance of staying together and agree on how this will be done. They must also more carefully assess physical differences and discuss how such differences will be managed.

ADAPTING PLANS TO DEAL WITH PHYSICAL DIFFERENCES

To manage physical differences constructively, group members must be able to accurately assess each person's abilities and effectively communicate about how physical differences will be dealt with. Well before an activity begins, each member should be clearly informed about the physical requirements of an activity. Each person should then be asked about specific physical activities or training that suggests he or she will be able to complete the outing as planned.

If it is apparent that an activity will likely exceed the abilities of some members, two courses of action can be taken. One option is to modify the plans in some way so people of different abilities can still participate but in slightly different ways. For example, a group might go to an area with several different trails, thereby allowing some members to select a longer hike while others choose a more leisurely route. If trails are selected well, it is often possible for everyone to leave and return at about the same time even though the actual routes may have been much different. On river trips it is sometimes possible for members who are less fit or technically skilled to meet their partners at some point along the river, thus allowing them to paddle a shorter distance or an easier section.

It is important to note that in these examples, the group is deciding together and in advance that some members will do one activity while others do something different. This is not at all the same as unplanned separations.

Unfortunately, it often happens that in an effort to keep groups together, well-meaning partners encourage their companions to go beyond their ability or comfort level. Comments such as "c'mon, you can do it" or "it's easy; we did it in three hours last time" are usually intended to inspire confidence. That may seem like a supportive gesture, but if such encouragement is not accompanied by an accurate appraisal of people's abilities it may turn out to be a regrettable mistake.

I have been on several trips in which the very people who were most vocal at encouraging friends to come along were also those who complained the loudest when those same friends could not keep up. I have also been guilty of inviting unprepared people on activities that were beyond their abilities. After several unpleasant experiences, I now think twice before inviting people on activities and I talk much more openly about any concerns.

TALKING ABOUT PHYSICAL LIMITATIONS IN GROUPS

In the course of assessing physical readiness, it will sometimes emerge that certain members of a group are substantially less fit than the rest of the group and may not really be in the kind of physical condition necessary to do the activity. Ideally, when the requirements of the activity and each person's fitness are discussed directly or are tested in practice through preparation trips, those who are not in shape will recognize that fact and will voluntarily opt out of that particular activity. If somewone who is not sufficiently fit does not voluntarily withdraw, others in the group may need to raise the issue.

If a group has a designated leader, that person should take responsibility for talking with people who are not up to a task. This is not easy, because those who would be "left behind" may have their feelings hurt or may not accept the leader's judgment. There is no easy way to deal with this situation, but it may be helpful to say something like the following: "Because I value our friendship, this is not easy for me, but I think we have to talk about the trip. I really enjoyed going on the hike last week, but it seemed you got very tired at the end. My concern is that the trip we have planned is quite a bit harder than last week's and to be honest I don't think it's a good idea for you to do it. I think you'd get exhausted and maybe hurt and that would put you and maybe everyone else in danger."

I have only had to take this step a few times, but so far it has worked out well. In fact, my anxiety leading up to talking with my friends has usually been much worse than actually speaking to them. In each case, although they were disappointed, they also knew that I cared about them and our relationship and that was why I was being honest. More than once people have confided that they in fact had doubts themselves, but were afraid to say anything because they didn't want to be embarrassed or to let others down. Talking together helped deal with those feelings and provide a positive way to address the situation.

The hardest part of this process, and what most people fear about speaking directly with partners, is what to do if someone insists on coming along even though it is clear she or he probably should not. A way to deal with this situation has two parts. First, speak with the person about the difficult position he or she is leaving you in. You might say, for example, "I know you really want to go, and it sounds like you think you can make it. This puts me in a bind because I have done this trip before and I know what it takes. To be honest, I really don't think it's wise for you to go. I don't want you to get hurt and I want to be fair to everyone else who is going."

If this still does not work, sometimes you just have to use your best judgment and tell someone he or she cannot go because he or she is not ready yet. This is a last resort, but it is better to risk offending someone before a trip than to risk the physical and emotional consequences that happen when people wear out in the middle of an activity.

Depending on the situation, you can communicate this by emphasizing that you are not saying people are not welcome on any activities, just that you are not willing to go with them on the specific occasions in which their physical conditioning is not adequate. If a friendship is real and strong, it should be able to withstand people speaking honestly with one another. If a relationship cannot endure such honesty before an activity, it will almost certainly not weather the frustration and anger that come from partners insisting they join activities for which they are not physically capable.

Thus, although it can be difficult to assess and discuss physical differences, in almost every case it is far better to deal with these matters directly and honestly. If physical differences are managed well, outdoor activities are more fun for everyone and relationship accidents are minimized. If physical differences are not addressed or dealt with openly, relationship accidents and other regrettable outcomes are extremely likely.

CHAPTER 5

EQUIPMENT

"Next time I borrow hiking boots from a friend, tell me to borrow some morphine too. And maybe a bone saw for field amputations."

"The guy in the store didn't say anything about the tent needing a rain fly. How were we supposed to know?"

JOHN MUIR, THE GREAT NATURALIST and founder of the Sierra Club, was fond of going into the wilderness with little more than a small satchel of food, a blanket, and the clothes on his back. For Muir, this manner of travel kept him close to nature and allowed him to move about freely, unencumbered by the weight of packs, tents, and other equipment.

Muir's example and achievements are impressive, but there are few people today who would be comfortable with his modest provisions. Although no amount of equipment can compensate for lack of skill or judgment, and too much gear can be as great an impediment as too little, the right equipment, used well, can substantially enhance the outdoor experience.

For outdoor relationships, equipment can influence the experience in a number of ways. Superior equipment can allow one person to perform beyond his or her partners, while inadequate or malfunctioning equipment can substantially reduce the enjoyment of those who must struggle with it. In some situations, inadequate equipment can be far more serious than simply a nuisance or source of conflict; it can endanger lives.

For these reasons, partners should give careful attention to their gear and should understand how the equipment may contribute to or detract from their outdoor experience and relationships. To help ensure that this issue is addressed adequately, as part of the preparation process, participants should verify the following:

EQUIPMENT CHECKLIST

- Each person has all the equipment necessary for doing the activity in safety and relative comfort.
- The person who will be using the equipment knows how to use and care for it.
- The equipment has been pretested and, if necessary, broken in before it will actually be used in the activity.
- All equipment is well adjusted for optimal performance.
- All critical equipment has been carefully inspected to ensure there are no weaknesses or flaws that could lead to failure.
- Team equipment needs have been coordinated, and shared equipment is equitably distributed among the members.
- At least a verbal (and, where necessary, an actual visual) equipment check has been conducted before the activity begins.

HAVING THE RIGHT EQUIPMENT

One couple described a time when they were first learning to white-water kayak. While playing on a wave, Bob felt surprisingly stable and was proud of his skill. Meanwhile, his wife, Alice, was nearby on a similar wave but was having great trouble staying upright. After tipping over several times, Alice said she was not having fun and decided to eddy out. Bob later admitted that he was upset at this, both because of what he perceived to be his wife's lack of skill and her lack of confidence and determination. "How is she going to learn if she doesn't stay with it?" he thought to himself.

A short time later, Bob went to shore and at Alice's suggestion they exchanged kayaks. When Bob went back out to surf, he tipped over even more than Alice had and eventually had to exit his boat and swim. Meanwhile, Alice was surfing like a pro in the other kayak. Enjoying the fun of being in control herself, she took no small sense of satisfaction in Bob's troubles and eventual swim.

Bob explained later that as he popped the spray skirt to swim, he suddenly realized the problem was not with Alice, it was merely a difference in the kayaks. He had the good fortune to start with a more stable boat, while she had started with a very tippy slalom model. Thus, what he initially thought was his greater skill was really just the luck of boat design. Of course, he had not realized or appreciated this until they exchanged boats and he found himself swimming.

Another example of the impact of equipment was provided by a couple who went backcountry skiing together. Mike was an experienced telemark skier, while his partner, Janet, had only tele-skied once before and did not own any of the equipment. On their first ski trip together, the snow surface was frozen solid. Mike and the rest of the party all had stiff telemark boots and skis with metal edges. Janet, however, was struggling with regular cross-country touring gear. Her low-topped boots afforded little control and the edgeless skis were almost impossible to turn. When the group reached a steep, icy slope, Janet realized she could not manage it and became frightened. This upset Mike, who, with greater experience and much better equipment, was not having any problems. When Mike yelled at Janet for being frightened, she began to cry and an argument ensued.

Discussing the experience later, Janet said she felt betrayed that Mike had not helped her get the proper equipment and had chosen such a difficult route under those conditions. Mike said he had thought

Janet was just not as skilled as he had hoped and he was very upset with her for crying instead of "toughing it out." This situation was made all the worse because until that point both Mike and Janet had felt they were a nearly perfect match and were thinking seriously about marriage. Those positive feelings were cast into doubt by this one very unpleasant experience.

Two critical lessons emerge from these examples. First, adequate equipment is very important. While the best equipment cannot substitute for skill and training, even highly skilled and well-trained people can be significantly impaired by improper or inadequate gear. Second, understanding the importance of our own equipment is the easy part. The more difficult task is to give the same understanding to our partners.

The most important "equipment" for successful outdoor activities and relationships will always be what we carry "inside." While it is essential that outdoor gear be reviewed and cared for and is adequate to the demands of the activity, we also need to attend to how we are dealing with that equipment and with one another. Awareness of our own needs and quirks, sensitivity to our partners, cooperation, flexibility, and a sense of humor can all help prevent problems with equipment from becoming problems with relationships.

In psychology, there is an interesting phenomenon called "the fundamental attribution error." This term means that when misfortune befalls me or I do not achieve my goals, I am likely to believe the reason is probably due to circumstances beyond my control. On the other hand, when misfortune befalls others or they fail to reach their goals, I am likely to assume it is due to some character flaw or lack of ability, not circumstances. Flawed reasoning, right? Of course, but most of us do it.

In the above examples, and in many other outdoor relationships, those with superior equipment are likely to attribute their partner's difficulties or frustrations to a "defect" in the partner as a person. From this premise a chain of criticisms or judgments can easily follow. "Gee, I thought she said she knew how to do this" or "He just isn't trying hard enough," etc.

To prevent such errors, it may help to keep in mind the old saying about "walk a mile in the other person's shoes." In the outdoors, if partners have defective or insufficient equipment, the relationship is helped if we can appreciate what they are experiencing. I literally had just such an opportunity when a friend's feet had become frostbitten and badly bruised during a climb. Because we had the same size feet and he was obviously suffering terribly from his boots, I offered to try exchanging boots for the final walk out. Wearing my newer plastic mountaineering boots, my friend reported an immediate improvement and his spirits noticeably lifted. For my part, I was able to finish the hike, but not without feeling a portion of the discomfort that had plagued my partner.

WHO OWNS THE TOYS AND WHY

It is also worth thinking about why differences exist in the equipment people have. Among the couples I spoke with, several reasons emerged to account for equipment differences. Two of the most important reasons were experience and money.

Over time, those who have more experience in outdoor activities tend to accumulate the necessary equipment (toys). Thus, more experienced hikers may have more than one backpack, sleeping bag, tent, pair of boots, etc., and can choose which gear to use depending on the length of trip, weather conditions, terrain, etc. Similarly, several people I spoke with had at least two pairs of skis, one old pair of "rock skis" and a newer pair for better snow conditions.

Contrast this relative wealth of equipment and options with the situation of the beginner or the less-equipped individual. While those with more equipment are able to select between sleeping bags, boots, and other gear, their less-equipped partners have to make do with what they have. Their equipment is rarely optimal for the demands of the activity, and they often have to make important physical and mental adjustments that their partners with better gear do not have to deal with.

Along with dealing with less than optimal equipment, the "equipment-poor" may also have to cope with less than optimal partners. A few people I spoke with were honest enough to acknowledge that they sometimes blamed their partners for equipment problems. Others confided that on occasion they actually took satisfaction when their partner's equipment did not function well.

Just as we may inaccurately attribute difficulties caused by equipment to inadequate skill, we may also attribute someone's relative lack of equipment to a personality or attitudinal factor. Often, a key reason for equipment differences is simply economics. Not everyone can afford all the toys for all the activities they would like to do.

To those who are either extremely dedicated to an activity or well-to-do financially, it may not be easy to appreciate the economic limitations to equipment. To the extremely dedicated, nothing is more important than the sport they love, so the sport gets first priority for both money and time. For people with plenty of money, dedication may not matter but they can easily afford to buy a brand-new set of gear costing $1,000 dollars or more, even if they rarely plan to use the equipment.

For the average person, outdoor sports may still be very important, but for the monthly paycheck there are also details such as feeding the children, health insurance, and house payments that contend with the local mountain or sport shop. One woman who was an accomplished athlete and certainly had all the grit and determination to do any outdoor sport was also a single parent of two teenage children. For her, one day of downhill skiing with the kids was a major assault on her budget, and buying new equipment, even at end-of-season prices, was entirely out of the question. She described countless times when she wanted to accompany friends skiing but had to spend the money instead on her kids.

This woman was not in any way asking for sympathy. Indeed, she was aware that such choices are an incredible luxury for many people in the world. Still, she felt her partner, a single and successful attorney with no children, did not really appreciate why she did not always want to accompany him to ski sales, and why she was willing to get by on eight-year-old secondhand gear. From her partner's perspective, her lack of interest in new gear was interpreted as disinterest in the sport that he loved and wanted to enjoy with her. When she tried to explain her financial realities, he honestly believed he understood. But his response was often something like, "Okay, I know. But look, these skis are normally three hundred and fifty bucks and they're on sale for two hundred. How can you afford to not buy them?"

If her partner really understood her situation, he would have understood how difficult it was for her to want to have new skis, and also to want to do things together but not be able to afford either. Further, when she was able to go with him on trips, rather than resenting the limitations of her equipment, he would have done better to understand and respect her efforts to balance the many demands on her budget.

PRETESTING AND BREAKING IN EQUIPMENT

Whether a person owns the most modern equipment or must rely on used or borrowed gear, before any outdoor activity it is essential that each person pretests and breaks in his or her equipment.

Failure to break in hiking boots is certainly one of the most common equipment-related problems and one of the easiest to prevent. The problem often originates in the store, when boots are purchased without testing to be sure they fit with real hiking socks, and without being certain that toes do not jam up against the end on downhill slopes. Of course, there is no way to equal a full day of hiking while testing boots in a store, but it is possible to wear the same kinds of socks one will use on the trail and to test proper fit by standing on inclined surfaces or kicking the toes into the floor. It is also a good idea to wear the boots for at least fifteen minutes to a half hour as you walk around a store. This may seem like a long time, and one might feel embarrassed about wearing the boots for such an extended period, but fifteen minutes is nothing compared to what one will actually do in the field.

The time spent trying out boots in a store is by no means the end of the breaking-in process. Once boots get home, they should be worn around the house for several hours. This gives further time to adjust the boots to your feet, and vice versa, while still keeping them sufficiently clean that there should be no trouble returning the boots. If things still feel good in the house, further testing can include walks around the neighborhood. Or perhaps you could follow the example of one man who walked five miles to work in plastic climbing boots with a fully loaded pack, complete with ice axe. A somewhat less extreme but equally effective method was used by a woman who wore her boots while mowing her lawn for a month prior to a climb.

You might feel silly wearing boots around the house or neighborhood, but before letting such concerns dissuade you, it is worth asking what it means if self-consciousness keeps you from doing whatever is necessary to ward off blisters and other injuries. One must also ask if it is fair to one's partners to make them wait while you stop to treat blisters or other problems that might easily have been prevented with forethought and a willingness to prepare.

One couple I spoke with said that at the start of every backpacking season, one member religiously wears boots around the house and goes for walks to break them in and get his feet used to them. In spite of this personal example and repeated encouragement, his partner never really prepares his feet before a hike. Inevitably, on their first few trips of the year, the one who prepared has few if any problems with his feet. Meanwhile, his partner suffers painful blisters that slow their progress and reduce their enjoyment of the trip.

New and poorly adjusted backpacks are another frequent source of difficulty. The first time I climbed Mount Rainier, I purchased a new backpack specifically for the climb. At the time, the pack was at the leading edge of technology and had the capacity to carry more things than a yak train of six. It felt great during the ten minutes I tested it in the store but on the hike to Camp Muir, I was more tired than I had ever been on a climb. After arriving at camp completely exhausted and doubting I could possibly make it the next day, I decided to try an experiment and test my friends' packs. Secretly, I hoped they were carrying lighter loads and that would be an explanation. No such luck. They were carrying just as much weight, if not more. Yet, in spite of that weight, their packs felt far more comfortable than mine. The next day, I left my expensive new frame pack at camp and carried a lighter summit pack to the top with no problems.

From that experience, I learned how important equipment can be. That is, I almost learned the lesson. In fact, I had invested so much money in the pack that I carried it for two more years, each time experiencing the same agony. Eventually, it got so bad that I almost quit hiking because I always felt so hammered and fell so far behind my friends. Looking back, that pack was a sort of store-bought Chronic Fatigue Syndrome.

Other equipment that is often not tested sufficiently beforehand includes tents, stoves, crampons, ski bindings, and any gear that requires assembly or adjustment. If you've ever watched as people try to put up a tent for the first time in the dead of night, a pouring rain, a howling wind—or all of the above—the value of having tested the process several times in the comfort of a living room is immediately apparent.

Tents can break and blow away, but improperly used stoves can set your whole place on fire. In the dim light and numbing cold of a climbing shelter, I once tried to light a new stove with the burner facing upside down. I might have burned the shelter to the ground if it had not been so cold that the floor was covered with ice and another hiker, no doubt fearing for his life, gently pointed out my error.

Adjustable equipment also plays into numerous problems when

it is not prepared before a trip. More than one climb has been aborted because crampons were not fitted until base camp, whereupon it was discovered that the needed tools were not available or small screws were broken and could not be replaced. Similar occurrences apply to ski bindings, kayak foot pegs, bicycle seat posts, etc.

There are plenty of unavoidable circumstances to cause outdoor relationship accidents, but blisters, improperly pitched tents, and even upside-down cook stoves can all be avoided. It's a lot easier to get along with our partners if we aren't fighting the pain of blisters or fighting fires in tent floors.

INSPECTING EQUIPMENT

Sometimes the problem with equipment is not a failure to break it in, but breaking it in so much that something has finally broken down. Even the highest-quality gear eventually wears out, but we can usually discover early warning signs by inspecting equipment before and after each activity.

One hiker told how the day before what was to have been a five-day camping and climbing trip, he discovered there were only a few stitches left holding the shoulder strap to his pack. Further inspection revealed that the hip belt was also about to go, as were some internal stabilizing straps. By discovering these flaws before the trip, he was able to go to a nearby shoe repair shop and have the weakened parts re-stitched. Had he not done this, there is no question that the pack would have given out somewhere during the trip. Hiking out with just one shoulder strap to support a heavy pack would not have been a picnic and it could have spoiled the trip for his companions.

To prevent equipment breakdowns in the field, it is a good idea to inspect all of your gear before and after each outdoor activity. To use backpacking as an example, start with the empty pack and look at all the straps, pockets, zippers, buckles, etc. The sleeping bag and tent are next: test the zippers, look for any obvious tears or weak points, and be sure all the tent poles and stakes are intact. Cook stoves should also get a once-over, with special attention to the gaskets on the fuel bottle. I learned this measure the hard way after an expensive tent was ruined by leaking fuel from a broken fuel bottle gasket. The gasket would have cost only a few cents to replace—the tent cost two hundred dollars. Water bottles can be checked by filling them and tightening the lids, then squeezing or standing on them gently to see if air or water comes out the top. A little water leakage probably won't ruin anything, but it can soak a sleeping bag and make for an unpleasant sleep. Leaking sports drinks make things even less enjoyable.

Other pre-checks include flashlights and batteries, with special attention to ensure that the bulbs work and fresh batteries are turned backwards until use so they are not inadvertently drained in the pack. Each item of clothing should also be examined, and details such as buttons on pants and laces on hiking boots should not be overlooked. Finally, though they are not part of backpacking equipment per se, it is always a good idea to be sure that vehicles have gas and oil, the tire pressure is correct, and other maintenance is up to date.

All this may sound compulsive, and perhaps it is a bit. Nevertheless, hard experience suggests that a little time and attention before an activity can save a great deal of frustration and discomfort if something breaks on a trip when there is no way to repair or replace it. Beyond discomfort or frustration, the importance of gear inspections becomes paramount when lives depend on equipment. Frayed climbing ropes, broken crampon straps or adjustment screws, cracks in canoe or kayak hulls, and other such flaws can cost parties much more than a good time.

Being in successful outdoor relationships means everyone attends to personal equipment well because they know their enjoyment, and sometimes their lives, depend on equipment being tested and prepared. If each partner has performed thorough checks on personal gear, the likelihood of an equipment failure is lessened for the whole group. I now routinely ask each individual I travel with if he or she has checked all equipment before we leave. If the answer is not a confident yes, and the nature of the activity is such that equipment failures could pose serious problems, I am not at all averse to taking a few extra minutes to go through the check together before we start up the trail, down a river, or wherever else we may be going.

FAMILIES
THE RIGHT GEAR FOR KIDS

Choosing the right equipment for families poses unique but not insurmountable challenges. One challenge involves getting equipment that fits children. Although it might be tempting to "make do" by using adult gear for kids, think twice before doing so. Remember how important first learning experiences are to later enjoyment. If children are forced to try to learn with gear that is too large, too heavy, or in some other way unsuited to their needs, they are likely to have far more problems than they would with optimally sized equipment. Having equipment that is the right size for children can save the children and their parents hours of frustration, whining, and other unpleasantries.

Fortunately, most of the leading outdoor supply stores and catalogue distributors now carry lines of clothing and other equipment in children's sizes. In many cases, kids' equipment is priced well below that of adults, but if a family is large, the costs can be prohibitive, especially given how fast children grow out of things.

Renting, rather than buying equipment, is generally a wise idea with children. It saves money up front and if the child does not take to the activity, parents have not invested a great deal of capital in further garage clutter. Another option that many parents rely on is to buy or borrow equipment used by friends with their children. Many schools, community organizations, and outdoor clubs have equipment swaps where children's clothing, skis, and other equipment can be found at inexpensive prices. Yet another successful approach is to post signs on outdoors shops' bulletin boards.

Finally, many parents sew clothing for their children. Patterns for simple pants, parkas, gloves, etc., are available from fabric stores or can be copied from ready-made gear. It is also possible now to purchase pile and other material in sufficiently varied colors to please almost any child. I still own and use a mountain parka that my mother sewed for me when I was sixteen. Knowing that she made it, and included a few custom features, makes it not only functional but also a cherished part of my equipment. When the wind is really screaming, I'm sure I get a few degrees of extra warmth knowing I am protected by something made with my mother's love and skill.

CARING FOR FAMILY EQUIPMENT

Owning the right equipment is a start, but knowing how to use and care for it are equally important. Parents who set good examples and involve their kids in pretesting, checking, and maintaining equipment instill habits that benefit children and their partners for years to come. This also enhances the immediate enjoyment of the children, as they feel honored by being entrusted with responsibilities. In one family, each child is given the job of checking a certain piece of equipment and is taught how to do so by a parent. The responsibilities are rotated on each trip, so each child eventually has experience testing each piece of equipment.

This same family also makes sure to pretest their equipment during trial expeditions to the famous and challenging "Mount Backyard." Before taking actual trips, they make a game of sleeping a night outside in their yard. Some creative storytelling and role playing by the parents gets the children involved, and everyone has a good time. They have even gone so far as to spray the tent roof with a garden hose as they shake it vigorously to simulate rain and wind. The kids love it, and when they get to the real outdoors everything feels much more familiar.

GROUPS

As the number of people involved in an outing increases, the potential for equipment-related relationship accidents grows exponentially. This is because each person carries multiple pieces of equipment, any or all of which could malfunction. What's more, as additional people come along, the chances increase that someone will not maintain or know how to use his or her equipment properly.

MAKE NO ASSUMPTIONS ABOUT EQUIPMENT

Because more people mean more chances for things to go wrong, it becomes even more important to attend carefully to equipment issues before the activity begins. A rule that I have learned after numerous disappointing experiences is "*do not assume anything!*" Even if people give you assurances that they know what they are doing and know just what to bring, make sure you check so you know that everyone has the necessary gear and it is in usable condition.

I was once on a climb with people who assured me they had good experience and knew what they were doing. Because we had previously done several hikes together and had talked extensively about the requirements for this climb, I assumed everyone knew how to dress for the conditions and would have the proper extra gear. Standing on a glacier at 13,000 feet, with still air temperatures near zero and a sixty mile-per-hour wind, we discovered that one of our party was dramatically under-dressed for the conditions and had brought along no extra clothing. Although this individual had spoken generally about having camped and climbed before, he underestimated the seriousness of the mountain we were attempting. As he began to shiver uncontrollably, the entire group was forced to stop in a rather unstable crevasse zone to take care of him. Had it not been for the extra clothing brought by the rest of us (those Ten Essentials made a difference), hypothermia would undoubtedly have set in very soon. As it was, we were able to get our companion warm again and we made the summit that day. That experience, however, taught me a valuable lesson about making assumptions.

EQUIPMENT CHECKS

To avoid repeating these kinds of mistakes, written equipment lists should be distributed in advance to each member of the group. These lists should then be discussed together so everyone knows what each piece of equipment is and why it should be included. Equipment lists and pre-trip discussions are particularly important when beginners or novices will be along, because items that experienced members take for granted may be completely unfamiliar to beginners. Further, to be consistent with the principle of not making assumptions, even if someone claims to already know everything needed, it is still a good idea to review things just in case.

If conditions on an activity will be particularly demanding or involve significant risk, mere discussion of equipment is not enough. In addition to giving lists and talking about gear beforehand, a physical check of equipment should be conducted before people get in their cars to start a trip.

One group of friends makes equipment checks fun by organizing potluck dinners several days before major outings. In addition to the dish for the dinner, everyone brings their equipment fully packed and ready to go. After dinner, they all go over what they have, test again to be sure everything fits or functions as it should, and share suggestions about how they pack, special ways of rigging gear, or other useful ideas. This way everyone in the group knows what their partners are bringing and that all the equipment has been well checked before leaving.

Such advance preparation helps reduce last-minute rushes that so commonly cause relationship accidents. If items are missing or need repair, there is time to do so before the trip begins. Reviewing equipment together also provides a way to keep weight within reasonable limits and equitably distributed. In many instances it is important that certain resources be accessible to the party as a whole, but that does not mean each person has to carry each item. For example, most parties should have at least one stove, water filter, first-aid kit, etc. If it is not essential for everyone to have each of these items, they can be distributed among members so the weight is reduced and shared.

A final yet very important reason for checking equipment together is to ensure that, in the event of an emergency, everyone knows who has what equipment. If critical items are needed quickly, being able to locate them rapidly could save lives. Further, if it happens that someone becomes separated from the group, knowing what equipment that person has can help in making decisions about possible searches or rescues.

WHAT TO DO IF PEOPLE LACK EQUIPMENT

The sticking point in group relations comes when people show up without the right equipment. This can be very awkward for group leaders and friends because they are torn between wanting a partner to come along yet not wanting to jeopardize the safety or enjoyment of everyone else. Obviously, such situations demand a judgment call that takes into account the conditions that are likely to be encountered and what the effects of equipment limitations might be under those conditions.

As a group leader, my approach to dealing with this is to be rather direct. I do not expect that everyone will have state-of-the-art equipment and I recognize that there are many different approaches and types of equipment that work perfectly well. At the same time, however, if I believe someone's equipment is inadequate for our plans, I express my concerns and we work together to see if there is anything that can be done to remedy the situation. Often, other group members have spare equipment they are willing to loan. It may also be possible to buy the needed gear on the way to an outing.

If an easy remedy cannot be found and members are still lacking required equipment, the group has to make a decision. They may choose to go ahead without the equipment, modify the activity that had been planned, or tell those with insufficient gear they cannot come on that particular outing.

There is no guarantee your partners will be pleased by this or will accept a decision that they not come as a sign of sincere caring for their well-being and that of the group. But expressing your concerns beforehand is actually far more caring than letting someone with thin boots get frostbitten feet, or someone with a faulty tent spend the night getting soaked. In some instances, such experiences might be valuable learning opportunities, but if serious injury or a miserable time for the group could result, such lessons may best be deferred.

CHAPTER 6

REASONS FOR BEING OUTDOORS TOGETHER

"We'd been hiking together for years before we realized that we really do it for completely different reasons."

"Michelle goes for the nature, I go for the challenge, and that's okay. We've found a way to make it work."

THE FUNDAMENTAL REASON FOR PARTICIPATING in outdoor activities probably appears simple: "to have a good time." The trouble is that different people have different definitions of good times. Some have to achieve a goal to feel satisfied—others primarily enjoy the journey. There are those who say nature is in their blood, and there are others who go along just to please their partners.

Of course, it is possible to cope constructively with such differences, but for that to happen partners must be clear with themselves and with each other about their purpose and individual needs. This is not as easy as it sounds because most people have not really thought about why they do things themselves or why they do things with other people.

Tom, a man in his mid-thirties, described a series of relationship accidents that all boiled down to the fact that he and his partners had different reasons for doing things. This discovery came to him while skiing—the sport he loved most but had never successfully combined with a close relationship.

"I love everything about skiing," Tom said, "the physical challenge, the freedom, the gear, the beauty of winter, everything. I've never felt more alive than when I ski. The trouble is that I could never find someone who had the same intensity of feelings about skiing as I did. That's how it was with my girlfriends when I was in college and it's the same way now with my wife. I used to live for fresh powder, but she hates to get up early in the morning. I like to tune my skis, but she thinks it's a waste of time if a shop can do it for her. Then there's the problems that happen because she doesn't ski as well. I've tried to be patient, but we always ended up fighting. We'd be standing there on the ski slope yelling at each other and I'd be thinking to myself, 'This is the one thing I come to skiing to get away from.' It was awful. I kept finding myself asking, 'Why the hell do I do this?'"

Tom had never stopped to answer that question until one day, in the middle of an argument on the slopes, Becky, his wife, told him directly that she didn't ski for the same reasons he did and that was okay. Becky said she was glad he got so much out of skiing and she knew it was important to him, but she skied just to have fun and to be with him in the mountains. The hard physical challenge, high speeds, and all the tech and equipment didn't really interest her.

Tom was at once dumbfounded, crushed, and enlightened—

dumbfounded because it had not occurred to him that his wife would not feel the same way as he did about skiing; and "crushed" because his illusions about how relationships "should be," how his relationship really was, and even his illusions about skiing as a meaning of life were all dashed by a simple, direct, and, worst of all, perfectly legitimate statement. At the same time, he was enlightened (though he confessed later that the enlightenment part was not immediately evident to him at the time) by discovering that it was not the end of the world or the relationship to understand and accept different reasons for doing things.

"I finally understood," Tom explained, "that it wasn't really how well we each skied or whether we got to the slopes early or any of that. What I'd really been wanting was for Becky to feel about skiing just like I did. When I finally understood, and could accept, that we're different, we were able to work it out. It seems so obvious, I know, but believe me it took me an awful long time to figure it out."

DISCOVERING WHY WE DO THINGS

Tom and Becky are by no means alone. Very few of the people I interviewed for this book had ever really discussed what they sought from their activities or why they wanted to do those activities with their partners. As an experiment to explore this further, I asked the members of several couples and families to write down a list of what they liked about certain activities and what they thought their partners liked. Just as Tom and Becky discovered, some of the reasons people listed were the same as their partners', but a surprising number were different. If you're interested in doing this with your partner, the exercise is presented below.

MOTIVATION REVIEW
1. Select an outdoor activity you do together, then write down some of the things you like most about it or some of the reasons you enjoy doing it. You might address areas such as the aesthetic aspects of an activity, physical elements, emotional elements, social elements, etc.
2. When you have finished writing what you enjoy about the activity, next write some of the things that could cause you to not enjoy it. Again, you might address certain aspects of the activity or events that you do not or would not like.

3. Now, repeat steps one and two but this time write down the reasons you think your partners do the activity and the things you think could reduce your partners' enjoyment.
4. When you have finished, exchange what you have written and talk about it.

Here is the list of reasons one couple provided for going sea kayaking together:
WK:

Getting away from all the hassles of work and home
Having a chance to relax
Enjoying the quiet of the water
Reading on the beach
Not having to be on a schedule

RL:

Having some time together with just the two of us
Exploring new places
Seeing the seals and other animals and sea life
Spending the day getting exercise outdoors
The adventure of being on our own away from all the
    usual comfort and security

These lists show that each person has perfectly legitimate reasons for why they sea kayak. At the same time, however, their lists and reasons are different in subtle ways that could easily produce conflicts. WK seems most interested in getting away from it all and having a chance to kick back and relax. From this list we can imagine WK's idea of a perfect trip as one in which they spend most of their time soaking up the sun on the beach. RL's list is a bit different. First, the primary reason listed is to spend time with WK. It is noteworthy that this reason was not among those on WK's list. Next, the remaining items of RL's list include more active pursuits, including such things as exploring, adventure, getting some exercise, and seeing a variety of animals and plants. Where WK's list suggests a relaxing day on the beech, RL's sounds like the ideal day involves a lot of time together in the kayaks paddling along the shore or between islands.

When we started this exercise, both people said they loved to go sea kayaking, but as we talked more about their reasons for going, they discovered that their ideas were more different than they realized. They also recognized that when they had argued during their last few trips, the arguments were precisely about these differences, but they had not realized it at the time.

Another way to appreciate why we do activities is to imagine removing certain aspects of the activity and see how we feel about what would be left. For example, you might ask yourself or your partner, "If this activity were not as physically demanding, would I still enjoy it?" or "If everyone else could do this activity, would I still be as attracted to it?"

When you imagine changing activities in different ways, you will probably find that some changes would enhance the activity for you or your partner, while other changes would substantially reduce your enjoyment. In talking with people, I found that conflicts often arose because one or both partners were not getting something from an activity that was important to them. They were often unaware of exactly what was upsetting them, but they knew something was not right because they were not enjoying themselves as much as they had hoped. Some examples of the kinds of changes that might alter enjoyment of an activity are listed below.

ACTIVITY PREFERENCES QUESTIONNAIRE

- If there were more people around, would you enjoy yourself more or less?
- If the natural surroundings were not necessarily "as beautiful," would you still do the activity?
- If the physical demands were higher or lower, would you be more or less attracted?
- If no one knew you did the activity, would you still find it rewarding?
- If the risks were different, either higher or lower, how would that affect your enjoyment?
- If you did not reach a specific goal, would you still have a good time?
- Does an element of competition increase or decrease your enjoyment?
- What other changes could enhance or decrease your enjoyment?
- Finally, and perhaps most troublesome yet potentially most important, if your partner were not along, would you enjoy the activity more or less?

You and your partners can undoubtedly come up with other possible changes or questions for yourselves. The key to making this process constructive is to understand that its purpose is not to "question" or make judgments about anyone. Rather, it is to better understand what each person seeks in an activity. This understanding will help your relationship and your activities together go more smoothly. It will also make it easier to talk about and resolve any problems that might arise. If you find yourself or your partner getting upset during an activity, try running the above questions through your mind to see if you can identify what is missing or present in the activity that is contributing to the problem. Once you identify that, you can adapt the activity to better meet your needs as individuals and as partners.

UNDERSTANDING WHY WE DO THINGS TOGETHER

In the Activity Preferences Questionnaire, the final question raised the issue: "If your partner were not along, would you enjoy the activity more or less?" This is a vital question for partners to ask themselves and one another. Unfortunately, the question is perhaps most likely to arise in the midst of conflict when at least one of the members may say to him or herself, "I don't know why we do this together. It would be better if (I, he, she, they) just went alone."

By the very nature of conflict, when we are not getting along with our partners we tend to focus solely on the current problem and, for that moment at least, we may be unable to think of a single good reason for being together. At such moments, it is usually much easier to feel the costs rather than the benefits of being together.

Instead of waiting until tensions reach the breaking point and the answers to why we do things together are so likely to be negative, partners can choose more positive or less stressful circumstances to talk about both the pros and the cons of sharing outdoor activities. Both the pros and the cons *must* be addressed. Simply saying, "Oh, everything is wonderful all the time when we are together" may sound terrific, but I have yet to meet a couple, family, or group in which there were not at least occasional tensions and drawbacks that accompanied the benefits of the relationship.

When drawbacks to doing something together are discussed, it can be helpful to keep in mind that the question isn't whether partners are "bad" or "good." More often, the real situation is that there is some specific behavior, or way in which the experience changes when you are together, that is at issue. By talking about how the experience changes when partners are together, and by identifying specific behaviors or other issues of concern, partners can work with one another instead of against one another to improve the situation.

The other critical thing to remember is that whatever drawbacks there may be to being together in the outdoors, there are usually more benefits. Thus, as we discuss things we would like to change in our relationships or activities, we should first identify what it is we enjoy about the other person and doing the activity with them. By thinking clearly about those reasons and keeping them in mind during your activities together, many conflicts can be avoided and those that do develop are much more likely to be resolved positively.

FAMILIES

Experiences as children can be critical to shaping the way we relate to outdoor activities and our partners as adults. In families, if parents assume that children do outdoor activities for the same reasons as adults, they are very likely to be disappointed when the children do not seem to be "having a good time" doing what the adults enjoy. Work-weary grown-ups may find great solace in sitting on a hillside letting time roll by with the clouds, but play-eager children will find that five minutes of time rolling by is pretty close to eternity. Type A personality parents may be driven to "reach the summit" or get to the destination, but children are more likely to be enthralled by finding that birds will eat peanuts out of their hands. As with adult partners, the point is not that the adult's needs are more or less legitimate or important than the child's. What matters is that we recognize, understand, and respect differences so we can respond to them constructively.

UNDERSTANDING WHY CHILDREN AND PARENTS DO THINGS

To understand the different reasons family members have for doing outdoor activities, we need to consider developmental differences in children's self-awareness and ability to express themselves. For example, children may not be able to clearly articulate exactly why it is they like doing something or why it is they are unhappy. They may simply express that they are happy or unhappy without knowing the reason.

When children indicate that something is wrong but are unable to clearly explain what upsets them, parents often find themselves experiencing a complex set of responses. Typically, parents begin with concern at the child's discomfort. But if the child cannot clearly identify the problem and the parent cannot determine what is the matter, the parent's concern may change to frustration. If parents then try several remedies without success, they are likely to become exasperated. If the situation escalates, conflict can result and what began as concern concludes in anger, with parents yelling or speaking sternly and children crying or whining. This unhappy but common sequence is played out hundreds of times each day at hiking trails, ski slopes, swimming pools, and other "recreational" settings.

If there is a positive side to such conflicts, it is that, in comparison to many adults, young children are much more direct about their feelings and are more capable and willing to adjust their moods as situations change. When children are upset, they usually let you know it directly. In contrast, we grown-ups tend to respond angrily inside and express it indirectly even as we tell our partners, "*No*, nothing is wrong!" Perhaps because children tend to be more direct, they also tend to get over things more quickly. Experienced parents know that a child who is crying and protesting one minute may be frolicking and laughing a few minutes later with no apparent aftereffects of the crisis that was just surmounted. By comparison, a fifteen-minute argument between adults can easily ruin a whole day or perhaps even a whole vacation.

To reduce the frequency of family quarrels in the outdoors, families who do outdoor activities together can set aside some time to go through the Motivations Review and Activity Preferences Questionnaire, talking directly with each person about what he or she likes or doesn't like about different activities. Ideally, this should be done when there is no pressure to go on an activity and when things are feeling positive in the family. Parents can present these exercises in a constructive light. For example, you might want to begin by saying, "I want to be sure we are doing things that everyone can enjoy, and that each of us understands what each other likes and does not like. That way we'll have more fun when we do things together."

For young children, the task of taking another person's perspective may not come easily, but by doing this with them, parents demonstrate that they think it is important to understand the needs of others. If children have trouble identifying the needs of others on their own, parents might help by offering suggestions like, "Well, what are some things your sister says she likes to do when we go camping?" or "If you really wanted to do something but found out you couldn't, how would you feel? That's kind of how your brother feels when . . ."

In spite of the initial awkwardness this process might produce, if family members really listen and try to understand each other, the benefits will become apparent as future outings begin to reflect the increased awareness of differing needs. Parents are also helping children develop a perspective and process that will not only aid the immediate family during its outings, but will also help the children avoid and cope more effectively with conflict when they are older and have families of their own.

GROUPS

Several years ago I accompanied a group of university students to study in Oviedo, Spain. While there, I learned of an organized outings program that arranged monthly excursions into the beautiful mountains and coastal areas of the region. Eager to enjoy this opportunity myself, and certain it would be a wonderful experience for the students, I made arrangements for as many students who wanted to to join a hike down a well-known and reportedly quite impressive canyon. When the day of the hike arrived and we met at the buses, I was chagrined and angered to discover that only five of the more than twenty students were there.

The next day I met with all of the students and strongly expressed my disappointment. I talked about how traveling was meant to be an adventure, and how one should grab every opportunity to experience new things, and how to live in Asturias without going to the mountains was a terrible mistake. When I finished my harangue, one of the students said that he was sure the hike was probably fun, but he preferred to spend that day having breakfast with friends. He continued to say that he thought I was out of order criticizing everyone as I had because it was not my place to tell them what they "should" like to do or how they "should be" as people.

Much as I hate to admit it, that young man had a good point. Each student had her or his own reasons for being in Spain, and their reasons were sometimes much different than mine. Whether I agreed with how they chose to spend their time, or why they did or did not do something, did not really matter. By wanting them to be different than they were and to share my sense of purpose and adventure, I was not changing anything. I was only frustrating myself and making them angry.

GROUP COMMUNICATION ABOUT INDIVIDUAL INTERESTS

When groups of people venture outdoors together, even though they may all agree to go together and do the same activity, each person has his or her own reason for being there and those reasons can sometimes clash. Unless we ask beforehand what people are hoping to get from an experience or why they are along, we may be caught off guard by such clashes.

Although it is seldom done, it would be quite easy for group leaders, or for each person in a group, to simply ask their partners what they are looking forward to about the activity or what it is they will most enjoy. With this information, all members of the group can work together to try to be sure everyone is getting at least something of what they wanted from the activity.

It is possible—indeed, it's very likely—that different needs or goals will emerge when people in a group talk about why they do things. It is also possible that expressing these differences will reveal certain tensions. This may be part of the reason groups don't have such discussions. But we should ask ourselves if differences are eliminated by not talking about them and if tensions are really reduced or conflicts avoided by not discussing different needs. We should also ask ourselves, "If a conflict might occur between group members, where is it best to happen? Well before the trip starts? Right in the middle after it's too late to turn back? When a crisis arises and we really have to work together but can't?"

Addressing possibly conflicting needs before beginning an activity may mean that plans need to be modified in some ways to make them work for everyone in the group. Talking about different reasons for doing something might also mean that some people will choose to not participate in an activity.

When the importance of understanding different needs is recognized, outings groups and activity leaders may feel they have been doing without something that they should have been carrying all along. Just as group leaders and members need to know that everyone has the requisite skill and equipment for an activity, it can be just as important to know the individual motivations and needs of each member. Such knowledge helps prevent problems and enables partners to work more effectively together for everyone's enjoyment.

CHAPTER 7

ON THE TRAIL

"No matter how good a trip looks when we plan it in the living room, once we get on the trail things seem to fall apart between us."

"Each time we go out, there are hundreds of little decisions that determine whether we'll have a good time. Deciding how fast to go, when to take breaks, and even how to talk to one another all make a difference. Make the wrong decisions and things can go bad; make the right decisions and everyone has fun. Sounds easy, but it takes a lot of work."

WHEN THE PLANNING AND PREPARATION ARE COMPLETE, the equipment's been checked and packed, and everyone's ready to go, it's time to head out. What lies ahead once we're underway? What sorts of relationship challenges and opportunities are likely to arise in the field? This chapter offers suggestions for how to keep the focus on fun throughout a trip. Dealing constructively with physical discomfort, fear, personal hygiene, competition, and safety are all addressed, as is the more pleasant topic of physical intimacy.

FUN CHECKS

One of the main reasons outdoor trips and relationships break down in the field is that people forget what they're there for. Because the ultimate goal of most trips boils down to having a good time together, it's important to find a way to make sure that's what's happening for everyone.

A quick and easy way to find out how a trip is going is to periodically take a break for "fun checks." These were described by an avid hiker who said that from time to time throughout the day someone in her group checks to see if everyone is having fun. Everyone in the group knows it's okay to be perfectly honest and, if something is interfering with the fun, the group works together to find a way to make things more enjoyable.

One example of a fun check that worked was on a group hike in which the pace was rather brisk and one member was really struggling to keep up. When the "fun check" time came, that person had a chance to say that yes, she was having fun but she would enjoy herself more if the pace were a bit slower. This information then led a few others in the group to acknowledge that they would actually like to go a bit faster.

The situation might seem ripe for a conflict and hard feelings but instead, because the group was primarily and sincerely committed to everyone having a good time, they found a compromise. Together, they looked at their maps and agreed that those who wanted to go faster could go on ahead at a quicker pace and use the opportunity to take a side trail that added some additional distance. Meanwhile, those who preferred a slower pace would cut back a bit on their speed and focus more on the vegetation, geology, and other surroundings. Before separating, they made sure that each of the separate groups had sufficient equipment to manage emergencies, and they talked about a contingency plan for what to do if their reunion did not happen as planned.

The key element to making fun checks work is for everyone to keep in mind that the real purpose of the trip is to have a good time and to accept that people have different ideas of what that is. If people speak openly about how the trip is going, partners can work together to find ways of ensuring that each person is getting at least some of what they hope for from the activity and no one is feeling like his or her needs or interests are being neglected.

An important point about fun checks is that sometimes conditions are such that even though members might say they are not having fun, there is not always something that can be done to completely remedy the situation. Nevertheless, it can be helpful to at least give voice to feelings and perhaps, if nothing else, share the misery aloud with one another.

A situation like this came up when weather forced a group of friends to abandon a planned climb and hike seventeen miles out through an incessant downpour. Everyone felt pretty miserable as they slogged through the quagmired trail, but they managed to conduct a fun check that proved to be important. A check of people's needs revealed that one member felt it would be good to take a quick break to refuel on gorp and water. After a five-minute stop to down some energy bars and much-needed liquid, it was surprising how quickly the group's spirits lifted. Although they couldn't make the experience the most "fun" trip they'd ever taken, they did manage to make it, as the Spanish say, *menos mal*— less bad.

CHECKING PHYSICAL CONDITION

The philosopher Descartes asserted that the mind and body are separate entities. Obviously, Descartes never did much hiking. It is a fine thing to think, as I have often heard, that "it is all in your mind," but pain and exhaustion can break the resolve and enjoyment of even the most stalwart outdoorsperson. What is more, and what we tend to forget, is that no person can really know what is happening physically to his or her partner.

If there is any truth to be found in the notion of mind/body dualism, it lies not in Descartes' vision, but in a reformulation that reads: "My mind may not be separate from my body, but it is certainly separate from my partner's body. Therefore, it is never possible for me to fully know what my partner's physical experience is, nor is it possible for my partner to fully know what my physical experience is."

This simple truth is extremely important because so many conflicts stem from people being unable to appreciate what their partners are experiencing physically. I have been on group trips in which one person said he was completely exhausted and his partner responded by saying, "No, you're not. C'mon now, let's get going." I have also been on trips in which a member was afraid to say anything about a developing injury because she did not want to stop the group and because she feared the scorn that stopping might evoke from her partner. The result was that a blister that could have been treated quickly and effectively with a patch of moleskin was eventually rubbed to the point of bleeding and such unbearable pain that the party had to turn back.

To prevent such problems, it has to be safe and expected for partners to be able to talk about their physical condition and make whatever adjustments are needed to stay healthy and safe and have a good time. This rule should be verbalized at the start of a trip and everyone should know that it is much better to speak up and make adjustments early than to suffer along until things get too bad to continue. It is also a good practice for partners to check with one another periodically as they hike and at each rest stop to ensure that everyone is doing okay physically. For those who might otherwise be reluctant to say anything, this provides a chance to respond if they need something.

In addition to checking on everyone's physical condition and respecting one another's needs, there are some basic steps that everyone should follow to reduce the likelihood of physical problems developing. Those with experience have long since learned these measures, but they may be unknown to neophytes.

PHYSICAL CHECKLIST FOR THE TRAIL

- Keep the pace within everyone's relative comfort limits. Going too fast early on exacts a high price later and easily spoils the fun.
- It is usually better to start a hike or other physical activity feeling a bit cool. Exertion quickly warms the body and by starting cool one can avoid having to stop to remove clothes. At the same time, however, if fifteen minutes or so of exertion still has not shaken the chill, it is then good to add extra layers to avoid heat loss.
- It is vital to take in plenty of liquid and nourishment along the way and to do so before one really feels very hungry or thirsty. This is

especially important in hot or dry climates and at altitude. A water bottle carried on the hip and easily accessible trail food make it much easier to stay fueled and hydrated.

- At rest stops, if some members have fallen behind, the early arrivers should not start out the minute the latecomers arrive. This breaks the group spirit and does not give those who are already more tired sufficient time to recover their strength.

- Blisters and other such irritations or injuries must be treated as early as possible. It takes five minutes to put on moleskin and get back on a trail, but untreated blisters that open can stop a trip entirely and make for a very painful return.

Because all partners in a group depend on one another, it is important that they all agree to follow these principles and attend to their own as well as one another's physical condition. One person told how a member on a climbing trip insisted that he did not need to drink as often or take in extra food as everyone else was doing. This insistence came in spite of the fact that more experienced members repeatedly urged him to eat and drink more. Predictably, midway through the climb this individual "bonked"—ran completely out of energy and became weak, cold, and somewhat disoriented. Fortunately, his companions recognized what was happening and quickly filled him with energy drink and energy bars, but it took a half hour or so for these measures to take effect and the climb was significantly delayed.

"If I had it to do again," said the person who related this story, "I would have just said, 'I don't care if you want to eat or drink more. I know what it takes to climb this mountain; you simply haven't eaten or drunk enough, and if you don't start taking in some fuel, I will not climb with you because you won't make it. It's that simple.' That probably sounds harsh," this person continued, "but I won't let myself get put in that position again. In those conditions, it's too dangerous and I'm not going to risk my life or anyone else's because someone insists on being stubborn or foolish."

The outdoors is not a place where one can afford to be unrealistic, and foolishness or bravado can be more costly than most people realize. To preserve one's own safety and to protect one's partners, it is literally vital to be very attentive and realistic about one's physical condition and to work together as a team to ensure that everyone stays as healthy as possible.

RESPECTING OUR PARTNERS' FEARS

There is a simple rule about fear that can make the outdoor experience much more enjoyable: *"Respect people's fear, whether or not you understand or feel it yourself."* There are lots of reasons to be frightened during outdoor activities, and partners should not have to feel ashamed or afraid of being afraid.

When someone is frightened, one of the least helpful but most common replies from partners is, "There's nothing to be afraid of." Whatever the intent of this statement, it is almost never of any use to the person who is frightened. It does not take away fear but it probably adds embarrassment and frustration to an already elevated level of stress. In all the years I have been in the outdoors, I have heard probably hundreds of partners tell their mates there was nothing to fear, but I have yet to hear the frightened person respond sincerely, "Oh, really? Thanks for explaining that. I feel perfectly fine now. The fear's all gone."

In the same way that one person can never fully know what is happening physically inside another person's body, no one can fully know another's mental experience. Simply because one person feels comfortable in a situation does not mean everyone else should feel comfortable as well. Top climbers may scale 5.10 pitches unroped and not feel fear, but beginners might be frightened on any exposed pitch, no matter how "easy" it might be rated. Similar differences in experience and fear can occur in any outdoor activity, whether it's skiing, white-water or sea kayaking, mountain biking, or even just a day hike. Rather than telling partners there is no reason to be frightened, or trying to encourage them to go beyond their comfort level, we need to first acknowledge and legitimize the fear, then work with those who are frightened to discover how they would feel most comfortable dealing with the situation.

I have long been appreciative of a good friend who taught me to kayak. As I was learning, he was always sensitive to my ability level and respectful of my fear. If we came to a drop that I was not comfortable with, he encouraged me to walk around it and did so in a way that allowed me to feel good. Typically he would say something like, "I think you're making a good decision. Anybody can do something stupid, but you could really get trashed and it just isn't worth it. I walked this place all kinds of times before I was ready to try it. If you aren't into it right now, that's cool."

Many times he would run the drop himself and we would meet at the bottom. On other occasions he would walk with me, not because he couldn't have done the rapid, but simply because he wanted me to feel okay about not running it. This was a superb example of how to deal with a partner's fear. My friend was willing to forego a run that would have been fun for him in order to be sure that I felt good about the experience.

Consistent with the rule of respecting fear, a corollary in climbing is: "If people want a rope, they get one. Period." A group described how they put this into practice while hiking on steep scree slope that dropped away above a long fall to a river. This was exactly the kind of place where someone might have said, "There is nothing to be afraid of," but the truth was that there was something to be afraid of: death.

Most of the group felt attentive yet comfortable crossing the slope, but two members were obviously frightened. Watching them start across the slope, one of their partners had a brief yet vivid image of how he would feel if the scree let go or the person lost balance and was gone. Without hesitation, he asked if the anxious members would like a rope and they appreciatively said yes. Rather than causing his partners to feel embarrassed, he created an experience that was positive for everyone. As a team, the group learned they could trust one another enough to be honest when someone is frightened. What is more, by crossing the trail with the security of a rope, the two members who had been frightened gained experience that made it easier for them to deal with similar situations in the future.

The dangers and fears that go with climbing, kayaking, or other risky sports are relatively easy to recognize and understand. But fears can also arise when dangers might not be so immediately evident or easily understood. For example, if parties become separated and members who are less comfortable in the woods end up hiking alone, they may be uneasy even though they are still on a perfectly well-marked trail. Similarly, if someone has not spent time outdoors at night, the sounds of animals or the darkness itself can be disconcerting. Even silence can be unfamiliar and in that sense troubling for some.

Eventually, just as ski runs that once intimidated us can become our favorites, other fears can be transformed into normal or even desired elements of outdoor experiences. This is most likely to happen if we have partners who are patient and supportive as we develop our skills and comfort level.

COMPETITION AMONG PARTNERS

For many people, competition is part of the fun of outdoor activities, but competition can also lead to relationship accidents. If a person feels that he or she always has to be in the lead or reach a destination before others, that person is less likely to be cooperative or supportive of partners. It can also happen that people assert they are not in competition, but if they find themselves lagging behind or not doing as well as others, they begin to play mental "games" to explain the situation. Examples of such thoughts, acknowledged by even very accomplished outdoorspeople, include:

"Well, of course he's going faster, he has a lighter pack."

"If I had equipment like hers, I'd be able to do even better than she's doing."

"I suppose if I had nothing better to do with my life than run rivers every weekend, I'd be able to do that drop too. But some of us have jobs and families."

"He's used to the altitude, so it's easier for him."

"I'm still tired after last week's trip. Otherwise I'd be in the lead."

This is not to say there's anything "wrong" with having such thoughts, and it must be recognized that each of them may be perfectly true. But the emotions and needs behind such thoughts are potentially quite instructive. To the extent that this kind of thinking reflects an underlying need to be superior to our partners, it may provide some insights into why we do certain activities the way we do them with our partners. It may also help us understand why certain emotions begin to emerge if our partners are more capable at something than we are.

During a discussion of this process with a group of women who often hiked, climbed, etc., together, several of them rather reluctantly admitted that they had just such thoughts at different times during their previous trips.

"Sometimes," said one, "we all know we are competing whether we've said anything about it or not. You can usually tell when that is and then I don't mind going all out. When it starts to bug me is if one person seems to be trying to get the best of the rest of us when we are supposed to be doing something just for fun together. I also hate it when I find myself resenting the others for doing better when I'm just having a bad day. Inside I know I'm being critical or petty, so I try to say, 'Now, relax, they're just doing better. Live with that and have fun.' That doesn't always work, but it's better than just stewing inside; at least if I recognize what I'm doing I can get over it faster."

As this woman spoke, her companions acknowledged that they had all felt very much the same way. They also said they felt relieved to be able to talk about it, as they had previously kept things to themselves and felt rather guilty. From this conversation, they reached an agreement to tell one another if they were up for a challenge and to speak up without losing face if they needed things to cut back a bit.

SEX

Most outdoor couples have their favorite stories about making love outdoors, and many can recount humorous tales about "getting caught," or canoes capsizing, or tents collapsing, or some other calamity. In spite of such hardships, the outdoors really can be a great place for romance. Without trying to offer a "Campers-Sutra," here are a few tips for the amorous.

First, consider safe sex and planning ahead. A couple I know spent a summer supervising a group of college students on a work crew building trails in California. Because there were a lot of students and provisions had to be brought in by pack animals, my friends kept close track on their stores. Near the end of the first week of a two-week detail, they took inventory and became aware that the plastic sandwich wraps they used for lunches had mysteriously disappeared. At first they suspected raccoons, crows, or other such varmints. But nothing else had been touched. Rather angrily they confronted their charges and demanded to know what was going on. No one stepped forward immediately, but the next day on the trail one of the young men confided to my friend that he and one of the girls had developed a relationship and, well, . . .

Avoiding the tempting jokes that this story invites (my friend swears it is true), one has to compliment the young couple for their awareness of safe sex and for their resourcefulness. But things might have been a bit safer and their intimacy more pleasant if they had used a bit more forethought. Throw a few condoms into the first-aid kit for good measure. They don't weigh anything to speak of, but if the opportunity arises, you're prepared.

Hygiene is another factor to consider in regard to sex and the outdoors. To be frank, sex can get rather messy. That's not so bad if you can hop in the shower and change the sheets, but if you'll be in the same tent or sleeping bag for the next week and happen to be on a "primitive" trail that doesn't have showers along the way, you and your partner will have to give some thought to cleanliness. Washcloth, soap, and towel can come in handy. Some couples also are selective about particular practices with a mind to hygiene. And remember that sexual activity may aggravate bears; this subject is discussed further in Differences in Anatomy, chapter 9, Men and Women.

The final point to be made here is that if the rest of the relationship is not working, sex, wherever it takes place, is likely to suffer too. That doesn't mean that if the tent is not always busy, the relationship is on the rocks, but it does mean that if partners cannot get along during the day, they shouldn't be surprised if things don't happen like magic at night. This might sound obvious, but as a therapist I've talked with hundreds of couples and it's amazing how many folks don't seem to understand there's a connection.

FAMILIES

The link between physical and emotional well-being is of special importance for children. Compared to adults, children are more vulnerable to fatigue, temperature, and other physical factors and they are often less able to deal with discomfort without becoming cranky. This means adults need to monitor how their children are doing and anticipate problems before they develop. At the same time, however, parents must walk a fine line between monitoring how their children are doing while not getting into conflicts over control and independence. The trick is to find a way to involve children in the process and create structures that make taking care of physical concerns easy, expected, and fun.

One way to help ensure that things go well for kids is to follow the previous suggestions regarding pace, eating, and drinking along the way, rest stops, etc. Because children may not be aware of the need to eat or drink before becoming hungry or dehydrated, parents should avoid asking the children if they want something to eat or drink. Instead, parents should explain before the trip starts that everyone needs to eat and drink regularly, so they will all be stopping every thirty minutes or every hour (depending on the age and ability of the children and the demands of the activity) for snacks and drinks. This works best if the children are enlisted as aids and given some responsibility for monitoring the time and helping make sure everyone, including themselves, eats and drinks.

It also helps to have along a variety of foods and beverages that kids like. Again, involving kids in the planning stage by asking what kinds of snacks they enjoy can reduce the frequency of "I don't like that" protests.

Along with anticipating the kinds of physical needs that children experience, it also helps to anticipate their emotional needs and the kinds of interpersonal conflicts that arise between siblings. Competition is a common source of conflict among children and many parents do not know how to deal with it well.

To positively resolve competitive situations, consider what a child is trying to achieve and what competition means for each child. For example, sometimes a child might compete with a sibling or friends to gain parental approval for his or her abilities. Other times, the child may be bored and trying to engage a sibling as a way to spark some action. Children may also use competition as a way to test their own abilities. Whatever the purpose, if parents begin by trying to understand the child's needs, they will be more able to find ways of meeting those needs without conflict and without the competition becoming a situation in which one child wins at the expense of the others.

Some parents maintain that competition between siblings is a healthy thing, and in some situations it probably is. In the outdoors, however, if an activity involves winners and losers, parents should not be surprised if the loser feels unhappy and those feelings come out in other ways during the trip. Parents should also understand that winning and losing may mean very different things for different children.

A close friend, who has a brother just a year younger, told me how as a child he always seemed to be in competition with his younger brother. "The trouble was," explained my friend, "there was no way I could really win. If I did something better than my brother, he could always say it was just because I was older. If things got too physical, I would get in trouble for picking on someone smaller than myself. But if he did something better and was able to beat me, I not only lost but had to suffer the indignation of losing to someone younger. It was a real catch-22. I don't think my parents ever really understood it, but that was part of the reason I never wanted to do outdoor things with them. Whatever we did always turned into a contest and I was bound to lose even if I won."

As an alternative to "win-lose" competitions, some parents find ways to invest children in challenges in which everyone wins. For example, seeing who can spot a deer or find a certain wildflower can capture the children's attention and channel a sense of competition in a constructive direction. As a variation on this approach, children can be given personal goals to achieve that are independent of what their siblings do. Thus, one child might be assigned to look for ground animals, while another looks for birds. This way whenever someone spots something everyone wins because they can all see it together.

SPACE FOR "THE GRUMPIES"

Another thing to keep in mind when doing things with children: It isn't necessary for everyone to be happy all of the time. Sometimes the best thing one can do is let it be okay for a child or someone else to just be grumpy. Parents who take children outdoors know that trying to keep kids continually satisfied or entertained is a game one cannot win. No human, adult or child, is always cheerful, so we need to give people space and time to get over things.

Experienced parents know that in most instances periods of whining, complaining, etc., pass and the child who was in tears one minute can easily be laughing and playing the next. On the other hand, if a parent feels compelled to meet all of the child's wishes or solve whatever might be troubling a child, that parent will quickly drive him or herself—and eventually the child—nuts.

A HAPPY ENDING

The effectiveness of applying these ideas was demonstrated by a young couple who went cross-country skiing together soon after they met. Both loved the outdoors and had met one another while downhill skiing. Although their downhill skills were about equal, when it came to cross-country Robert was much more experienced, having competed in races of fifty kilometers and more. Kristin was concerned about whether she could keep up, but she didn't want to express any concern for fear of upsetting their relatively new but promising relationship.

Once on the trail they soon discovered that the difference in abilities and conditioning was much more than either had expected. Kristin found herself falling behind and Robert was frequently much farther ahead of her than he realized. He tried to wait patiently and Kristin tried her best to keep up, but the exertion took its toll and she began to get upset with herself, Robert, her skis, the snow, and everything else that was conspiring to wear her down. In less than an hour she felt utterly exhausted. At their first rest stop, Robert told her they still had several hours to go. As tired as she was, that news was very disheartening to Kristin. She tried hard to cope well, but felt like she was going to cry.

At that moment, it was looking like another relationship accident waiting to happen. Fortunately, both people did things that turned potential disaster into a pleasant experience. Kristin decided she should say how she was feeling physically and emotionally. As she explained later: "I realized it was silly to just sit there and feel miserable to try and impress this guy. If he couldn't understand how I was feeling, it probably wasn't worth the trouble anyway." At the same time, Robert noticed that Kristin was looking tired and upset and he asked how she was doing.

"To tell you the truth," Kristin said, "I'm really tired and I'm feeling pretty bad." Robert listened without becoming upset and Kristin was then able to say that she had serious doubts about being able to reach their destination. Much to her surprise, Robert said that was fine. He acknowledged that he had probably picked too tough a route and apologized in a way that was genuine and did not make Kristin feel bad. Robert then asked what Kristin would like to do. Following a discussion of their options, they decided to turn back at that point and follow easier terrain. This was a great relief for Kristin and she had a wonderful time during the rest of the day. A few months later they became engaged and they continue to share outdoor adventures to this day.

CHAPTER 8

TEACHING AND LEARNING WITH PARTNERS

"Just once I'd like to do something without my boyfriend feeling he has to teach me how to do it."

"I do my best to help him get better, but he is so stubborn sometimes I think it is impossible to teach him anything."

WHEN ASKED ABOUT WORKING WITH COUPLES, a young instructor at a kayaking school told me, "We have a policy to always place partners in different classes from each other. We also tell them to not try to teach each other anything. Just leave that to us." The same instructor added, "I even do that with my girlfriend. I always let one of the other instructors teach her. For some reason, I can get along with almost all of my students, but when I try to teach my girlfriend, disaster strikes."

It is natural for people with more experience to teach those with less experience. This seems like such a reasonable arrangement that one might wonder how anything could go wrong. But the dynamics of teacher-learner roles were acknowledged as a source of conflict by almost everyone I interviewed.

The inherent conflict was perhaps best illustrated by two people who were both instructors in different sports. Each was known to be an excellent teacher, and both had been very successful working with students of all types, including those with physical disabilities. When it came to their own relationship, however, they found themselves totally incapable of teaching or learning from each another.

"It's really amazing," Linda said. "One day I can spend three hours working with a kid who, after all that work, can still barely stand up on skis. But the next day when I try to teach Ted, in ten minutes we're fighting and in fifteen we've given up."

"It's the same for me when we're windsurfing," Ted added. "A couple of weeks ago I had a great time teaching a guy who was blind. But with Linda, I got so frustrated that the last time I swam to shore and left her with the board."

What this couple has eventually come to accept is that teaching or learning with others is much different from teaching and learning with partners. For those who by choice or necessity find themselves teaching or learning from partners, understanding certain underlying issues can make a remarkable difference in heading off relationship conflicts.

KEY CONCEPTS FOR TEACHING OR LEARNING WITH PARTNERS

- Understand the vulnerability of partners who are learning and teaching.
- Understand the power issues inherent in teaching and learning.
- Understand role imbalances that contribute to and result from teaching and learning together.

- Appreciate your limitations in skill at an activity and as a teacher of the activity.
- Recognize that it takes time and practice to learn. Don't go too fast or try to do too much.
- For many people, it is much better for the relationship to take lessons from a professional instructor rather than from a partner.
- In families, find ways to do activities so family members don't always feel they have to teach or learn from each other.
- In groups, avoid having everyone try to teach simultaneously.
- If you are not specifically recognized as being in the role of teacher, ask "permission" of the learner before offering suggestions.
- Whether you are in the role of teacher or learner, consider the guidelines at the end of this chapter and try to put them into practice.

VULNERABILITY

The first thing to understand about teaching, learning, and relationships is that conflicts are not solely due to how or what one person is teaching another. Rather, conflicts result in large part from the roles each person is filling and their emotional reactions to those roles.

Even if you are an expert teacher, it is not always easy to appreciate the emotional needs or responses of your partner as a student. Because teachers want their partners to learn quickly so they can enjoy an activity together, it's easy to become frustrated if progress isn't as fast as the teacher would like. At the same time, those in the role of learners may feel resentment for their partners' greater facility with the activity and for their partners' apparent lack of understanding and patience.

An almost universal feeling for the learner is the sense of vulnerability. Anytime we try something new, we make ourselves vulnerable. We are vulnerable to failure, frustration, sometimes to physical risks, and, most importantly, to evaluation and loss of self-esteem in front of others.

One beginning climber told me that learning from his wife how to tie certain knots made him feel just like he had when he was a child and his brother was trying to help him with his algebra homework. "It's the same way with knots," he said. "She can make it look so easy, but when I try to tie them I get so confused I want to bag the whole thing. It really drives me nuts."

Just as students feel their self-esteem is on the line, teachers also feel that their abilities are in question if partners aren't learning. If those in the role of teacher can't come up with the right clues to help their partners learn, they may become frustrated with themselves and feel like they're failing as teachers. The result is that both people end up frustrated with themselves and with their partners and feeling like failures. Is it any wonder that relationship accidents happen under these conditions?

POWER ISSUES

It is often said that knowledge is power. If that is true, those who have more experience or knowledge of an activity are in more powerful positions than their less experienced partners. When I raised this possibility during interviews, people in the teacher role often shook their head and said they weren't out for power, they were just trying to help their partners. "In fact," said a canoeing instructor named Greg, "if anything, I'm trying to make Ed more powerful by teaching him."

In contrast to this response by teachers, the learning partners were much more likely to give a nod of recognition or insight. Greg's partner Ed replied, "I know that's what you want, and I appreciate it. But I do feel less powerful than you when you're better than me at something. I'm glad you teach me but sometimes when I don't learn as fast as you want, it makes me feel like a failure."

GIVING COMMANDS VERSUS OFFERING SUGGESTIONS

To better appreciate how the teacher-learner role involves power issues, think about the dialogues between teachers and learners. In the most typical scenario, the teacher tells the learner what to do, and the learner is expected to follow instructions. Statements like "bend your knees more," "lean into it," or "use your shoulders more when you paddle" may all be useful instructions, but there is a fine line between a suggestion and a command to do something.

In general, power issues are reduced and better results come for partners when those in the teaching role think of what they say as suggestions, not orders. If this is genuinely the attitude of the instructors, learners can choose to try the suggestion or not.

If it sounds strange for the person teaching to offer suggestions rather than instructions, that's because most of the teaching models we grow up with are based on power differences that probably shouldn't exist in relationships between partners. We all learned how to teach and learn from our experiences as students in school and from our parents. When a teacher or parent says to do something, the student or child is expected to do it. This relationship style and the communications that go with it tend to come out again when partners teach one another.

Ideally, our relationships should not be based on parent-child or teacher-student power structures, but on positions of mutual respect. If there are power imbalances in our relationships, thinking in terms of offering suggestions rather than instructions gives us the opportunity to change not only the interaction of the teaching situation and outdoor activity, but also the power dynamics of the relationship as a whole.

One couple had videotaped a session in which one partner was teaching the other how to play golf. Watching the tape again after our discussion, they were surprised to realize how almost all of the communication from the teaching partner was in the form of a command rather than suggestion. They also found that the person who was teaching at first had great difficulty coming up with any other way to instruct than by using commands.

If it's unclear whether power issues are involved in teacher-learner or other interactions, a good way to find out is to pay attention to how each person feels when an "instruction" is not followed or not followed "correctly." Does the person giving the advice become angry because the advice was not followed exactly? Does the learner feel satisfied for doing what he or she wants and not what the partner said? And, the key question, are issues about the relationship somehow getting in the way of or being exacerbated by the process of teaching and learning the skill?

As you discuss these issues with your partners, remember that if partners say they are feeling a certain way about an interaction, it is most productive to listen and try to understand the feelings. This may sound like an obvious thing to do, but instead of really listening a more typical reaction is to say the other person shouldn't feel hurt or angry because he or she didn't really understand what you said or did. Telling partners why they shouldn't feel the way they do is not very likely to change the way they feel, and it's almost sure to prevent your own understanding of what is going on. If we think about the learners, our partners, as people, first, then we think second about the lesson, they are more likely to feel good about the experience and will probably learn much faster.

ROLE IMBALANCES

It is also important to be aware of the overall nature of activities together. Partners often report that the roles of teacher and learner in outdoor activities tend to be one-sided. That is, one person tends to always be the teacher and the other the learner. Even if partners do their best to improve their interactions as teacher and learner, constant imbalance in roles, and the accompanying inequalities in vulnerability, power, and responsibility, pose difficult challenges.

THE LEARNER'S ROLE

Typically, though not always (and this, happily, is changing), men have more experience in outdoor activities than women. This means that in outdoor activities men are more often in the teaching role than women. This pattern is important to understand because it fits into a larger social context that brings different meanings and consequences to the people in a relationship. When gender differences emerge, the issue is not as simple as, "Well, one person knew more than the other, so that person was a teacher." Rather, the issue is more accurately represented as, "In our society, one gender is almost always given credit in advance for knowing more and is therefore given an assumed authority as a teacher."

This may be somewhat of an overstatement and, again, times are changing, but the subjective experience of many women is that they are consistently given less credit for their knowledge and abilities and that in turn places them at a distinct disadvantage. On the other hand, men are taught to feel like they should be skilled at everything. When men are not skilled or knowledgeable about an outdoor activity, they tend to feel like their masculinity is somehow at risk. This situation makes it extremely difficult for women to learn from men and for men to learn from women. More is said about the influence of gender differences in chapter 9, Men and Women, but it's worth raising at this point because it bears so directly on the issue of teaching and learning.

A woman named Trudy, whose partner, Ray, had helped her learn downhill and cross-country skiing, backpacking, and several other outdoor pursuits, said she loved everything they did and Ray was a very good teacher, but she began to feel like there was nothing she could do as well as him. He seemed expert at everything and she was a "klutz beginner." She went on to say, however, that there were some things she did better than Ray, but they almost never did those together. "I used to play volleyball and racquetball before I met Ray, but he never wants to play because I always win. I like to sew too," she continued, "and I tried once to teach Ray, but he was all thumbs and got frustrated. The next time I asked if he wanted to try, he said he wasn't interested and never tried it again. That was a change though, because before we started he'd said he wanted to be able to make and repair things on his own. When he had a hard time and saw that I could do something better, he quit." Finally, Trudy remarked, "If I was like that too, if I refused to do all the things we do that he's good at, we wouldn't do anything together."

When Ray heard Trudy's comments, he responded by explaining that he really didn't need to learn to sew because that was something you did by yourself and Trudy was so good at it already the family didn't need another expert. As far as volleyball and racquetball went, he "just wasn't into competitive sports."

On the surface Ray's response might sound perfectly reasonable, but it missed the point of what Trudy had been saying. By not doing things that Trudy enjoyed for herself and was good at, Ray was in effect communicating that he did not value those things enough to do them with her or learn them himself. What's more, he never had to fill the role of student and experience the kinds of frustration and vulnerability that Trudy faced on a regular basis in their outdoor activities. At the same time, Trudy never was allowed to be in the role of teacher and gain the satisfaction of helping her partner learn something. It isn't surprising that Trudy began to feel inferior not just as a skier or hiker, but as a person and partner. It's also not surprising that she was beginning to resent Ray for his role in fostering her sense of inferiority.

One of the interesting things about the experience of Trudy and Ray is that until we talked about it, they had not fully realized or ever discussed how their activities played more to Ray's strengths than Trudy's. They also had not realized how this imbalance affected and reflected other aspects of their relationship. Most of the partners I interviewed recognize that one person or the other tends to be the teacher or learner, but they haven't really thought or talked about what that means for their relationship.

THE TEACHER'S ROLE

The person who is usually in the role of teacher also has a difficult task. Teachers can become frustrated with their partners and with themselves when the partner doesn't learn something as quickly as both would like. Partners who are consistently teachers also feel the resentment and resistance that can come from learners and it isn't always easy to deal with those feelings. "It gets tiring to always have to be patient and supportive," said one. "I know he resents it when I keep giving him suggestions. I can feel it in the way he looks or little things he says. That's hard for me because I'm doing my best to help him learn. When he gets angry like that, I want to just tell him to bug off and learn it by himself."

Partners who fill the role of teachers also explained that by always teaching, they seldom have the opportunity to really go "all out" in their activities. As one man put it, "I'm always having to be the teacher. When we play tennis I teach, when we ski I teach, when we climb I teach, when we bicycle I teach. It never stops. Sometimes I just need to get together with someone who already knows how to do things so we can just let it rip and go all out without worrying about the other person."

Recognizing the stress that the continued roles of teacher and learner was causing on their relationship, this man and his partner agreed that every three or four times they would do the activity only with people of their own ability levels. That way they didn't always have to be teaching or learning or trying to go faster or slower to match each other. Both agreed this strategy works well and that taking some time away from one another makes it more fun when they are together.

A LITTLE KNOWLEDGE IS A DANGEROUS THING

Things are made even more difficult when partners who try to teach each another are not particularly skilled themselves and may in fact be teaching incorrect technique. And even if partners are skilled at an activity, that doesn't mean they're skilled as teachers. It's easy to say "just watch how I do it" or "bend your knees," but that may not be enough to help someone develop a skill. If a learner doesn't understand the instructions or has a hard time executing them, the teacher needs to have more resources to draw upon. Merely repeating the same instructions louder and more forcefully is unlikely to help someone learn.

By comparison, experienced instructors have large and tested repertoires of hints, exercises, games, images, etc., to help their students develop skills. For example, rather than simply telling someone to keep the upper body facing downhill while skiing, an instructor might suggest that the student imagine carrying a tray of teacups while facing down the hill and trying to not let the cups spill or fall off the tray during turns. This simple trick is remarkably effective at helping teach a quiet upper body and proper positioning. A person who does not know or use such teaching tricks can try unsuccessfully all day to accomplish something that may be easily achieved with a simple, well-timed concept or image.

PRACTICE TIME

Partners who are not experienced teachers also lack awareness of how students learn and progress through skill development. Inexperienced teachers tend to expect their partners to learn skills easily and progress far more rapidly than is realistic. This happens in part because people want their partners to develop skills so they can do things together. It also happens because inexperienced teachers don't realize how long it takes people (including themselves at one time) to learn skills.

The desire for partners to learn quickly is easy to understand, but the best intentions can create pressure that leads to exactly the opposite of the hoped-for results. The solution is to take away the pressure to learn quickly, allow time for practice, and, most importantly, focus on enjoying the learning process itself, not on achieving the final goal of a hoped-for ability level. Once again, principles from the Relationship Ten Essentials can come in handy. Patience, sensitivity, flexibility, etc., go a long way toward making learning and teaching with partners more enjoyable.

TEACHING AND LEARNING IN FAMILIES

Issues about teaching and learning are particularly likely to arise in families because of the inherent relationship and role differences between parents and children. Just as adult partners may tire of repeatedly filling the role of teacher or learner, similar issues apply to children and parents.

CHILDREN AS LEARNERS

A young woman named Angela was in her first year of college and a member of her campus outdoor group. When I asked about her memories of outdoor experiences with her family, she laughed and said, "You have to understand that I have two older brothers. For me, every time we did anything, it was 'teach Angie' time. I learned a lot from them, but sometimes I just wanted to say, 'Shut up and let me have fun. I don't want to always have to be taught by you.'"

Angela went on to explain that she wanted to learn, but she always felt so much pressure it seemed she was learning because someone else wanted her to, not for herself. "The trouble was that if I ever said anything like that to my brother, he would just get mad and say, 'Fine, sorry I bothered' or something like that and take off angry. Then I'd feel bad and guilty and couldn't enjoy myself. It really felt like a no-winner sometimes."

Similar experiences were described by many people. Typically, younger family members felt they were always the learner and older family members, either siblings or parents, were the teachers. In most cases, persons in both roles felt that at times the roles were burdens that interfered with enjoyment. Angela summarized the situation well by saying, "It got to a point where if my parents or brother asked if I wanted to go skiing, all I thought to myself was, 'Do I really want to spend another day being taught by my brother or parents?' Lots of times I said no even though I really did want to ski."

PARENTS AS TEACHERS

On the other side, parents report that feeling responsible for teaching children sometimes takes the fun out of activities for them. "We used to love to play tennis," said one father. "But once we started teaching the kids to play, we turned into "ball boys." Now we spend the whole time chasing balls around the court and over the fence, apologizing to other players, and on and on. I can't remember the last time I played a serious match."

A large part of the problem is that when parents or older siblings teach younger children, they carry over roles from other family activities into the outdoor situation. At home, parents tire of getting after their children to do their chores around the house, do their homework, take their dishes to the sink, etc. For their part, children feel like they're always on the receiving end of directions. When these same patterns are brought to outdoor activities, they don't feel much like a refuge or a break.

I once overheard a frustrated young adolescent say to his parents, "One minute you tell me I should take in the beauty of nature, and the next second you're on my case to tie my shoes, or tuck in my shirt, or not walk so fast. It's kind of hard to relax and look at nature when you're always telling me what to do."

Another issue that complicates teaching and learning in families is the fact that most parents have little training in how to teach. Parents are granted the "authority" of teachers within their family simply by virtue of being parents. But without training, and without explicit recognition and acceptance as a teacher by other family members, the parent who tries to teach is in an ambiguous position.

One remedy for such problems is for families to find opportunities for teaching or learning but also to allow plenty of opportunities to just do things without having a lesson attached. It's also important for kids and parents to do activities separately from one another and with people of their own ability level. Organizations often have activities specifically designed for people of different ages or experience levels. Schools are another excellent resource. If kids are involved in organized school activities, they get a chance to do activities with their peers and receive instructions from someone other than their parents.

SPECIAL ISSUES IN "BLENDED FAMILIES"

Teaching and learning problems are probably present to some degree in all families, but they may become more complex in "blended families," i.e., stepfamilies, adoptive families, and others in which the family structure may not have been in place for the lifetime of the children.

In one family, an avid outdoorsman had married a woman who had two teenage children from a previous marriage. When the couple married, they hoped their love of the outdoors could be shared with the children. However, as they tried to involve the children, they noticed that the oldest boy, who was sixteen at the time of the marriage, seemed to actively resist learning anything from his stepfather. When the stepfather offered suggestions, the boy was quick to respond that he already knew or that he had a better way.

This response hurt his stepfather's feelings and frustrated both parents, but they did their best to understand and be patient. As the stepfather explained, "I think I understand. For Todd it's not just about the activity or how I teach. It's really about his relationship with me in general. If he learns something from me, it probably feels like more of an emotional connection than he's ready for just yet. I think he feels like he's betraying his natural father if he gets close to me. I suppose my best strategy is to keep offering, try to not pressure him too much, and just be there if he needs or wants my help."

What impressed me most about this family was how the parents were doing their best to understand the experience of the children from the children's perspective. Although the children did not always show they appreciated efforts to involve them in activities, the parents continued to provide opportunities. The parents also allowed the children to participate in ways that left the children a degree of independence and identity. Whatever the family structure, this combination of patience, trying to understand the children's experience, and finding ways to respect the children's identity can be critical to both the immediate satisfaction and the long-term enjoyment of outdoor activities.

TEACHING AND LEARNING IN GROUPS

In groups, especially informal groups of friends, it often happens that no one is explicitly recognized as a teacher. This sometimes means everyone appoints him or herself to teach others, whether or not they really know what they're doing and whether or not the people being taught really want the instruction.

INFORMAL GROUPS—WHO TEACHES WHOM?

I once watched a group practicing basic climbing techniques in preparation for a summit attempt on Mount Rainier. It was evident that two or three members of the group had more experience than the others, but no one in the party was a trained instructor and no one had been specifically designated to teach the group. The result was a confusing combination of advice, some of it useful, much of it questionable, as every member of the party tried to teach simultaneously.

One man, who was having difficulty learning to self-arrest (use his ice ax to stop a sliding fall), received advice from at least five different people before one of his practice slides. The man was obviously nervous and it was clear that his companions all wanted to help, but the clamor of suggestions seemed to only add to the confusion and fear. In the process, the advice of the one person who seemed to most know what he was doing was quickly drowned out by the much less helpful suggestions of others. I wondered if anything useful would really be learned that day. I also thought to myself what might happen on the mountain if a real emergency arose and the group had to work as a team.

The interactions of the would-be climbers demonstrate several common dynamics of teaching and learning among groups of friends. When no one has been designated as a teacher or leader, everyone is eligible to fill that role whether or not they actually know anything or know how to teach. Under these circumstances, the factors that determine who will teach and who will learn are often determined more by personality characteristics than competency. Along with personality, gender roles also influence who teaches and who learns, with males tending to step in and "help" females whether or not the females need or want help.

This chaotic approach is certainly not the best way to teach, learn, or work together as a group. It can, however, produce some humorous moments. I once looked on in amusement as a man who was new to a running group offered unsolicited, and largely erroneous, advice about triathlons to a woman whom he apparently assumed knew little on the subject. It happened that the woman was in the top ten triathletes in her age group and had set numerous records throughout the region. She listened politely and thanked the man for his suggestions, but the next day on a group ride he discovered his mistake when she arrived with her ultra-tech bike and proceeded to hammer the legs off everyone.

TEACHING AND LEARNING IN ORGANIZED GROUPS

Organized outdoor groups typically offer more structured programs of training, with group members serving as instructors. This reduces much of the role ambiguity, but it doesn't eliminate the complexity of the teaching and learning process. Merely establishing a program of instruction and identifying certain members as instructors does not ensure that all instructors are well trained or that students will not question the competency of the instructors.

PREPARING INSTRUCTORS

Perhaps the most important principle for instructors to understand is that they do not have to know everything. Many organizations have members who are highly accomplished outdoorspeople and exceptionally skilled teachers. Nevertheless, there will inevitably be times when even the most experienced instructors lack certain knowledge or teaching skills. In such situations, the best strategy is simply for instructors to be honest about their limitations and be willing to ask other instructors for assistance.

Instructors can also be receptive to suggestions from students, but should take care that sufficient structure is maintained to avoid the "too many cooks" situations. One way to do this is to tell people that the designated instructors will complete their teaching sequence as they plan and they would like people to hold any suggestions until the instructor has finished.

Another problem that sometimes arises for organizations occurs when large classes are divided into smaller groups that are taught by different member-instructors. Under these circumstances, it is bound to happen that different instructors will teach the same skill in different ways. Because varying instructions can be confusing to students, it is a good idea to work closely with instructors and coordinate approaches before a class begins. It's also a good idea to tell students that by working with different instructors they have the opportunity to profit from the experiences of many individuals and that sometimes ideas will differ. As long as lessons are consistent about critical matters such as safety and essential technique, differing ways of teaching can be an asset rather than a liability.

REVIEWING INSTRUCTION AND DEBRIEFING

Instructors should also get together after each class to discuss how things went. This "debriefing" allows instructors who had difficulty teaching certain concepts or skills to ask others for suggestions. If the instruction is part of a series of classes, instructors may also want to use the debriefing time to discuss any concerns they have about individual students. The team of instructors needs to know which students are progressing well and which might need special attention. This process can be especially important if the activities being taught involve risks and if certain students might not have the necessary personal characteristics or skills to perform safely.

As instructors talk about a class or individuals, it's important to remember that the purpose of the debriefing is to help resolve problems and learn new teaching approaches. Debriefing is not an opportunity to make fun of students who are having trouble. A little good-natured story sharing can help alleviate frustrations, but this should always be in a context that seeks to find ways to help even the most frustrating and difficult students make progress.

HOW TO TEACH AND LEARN

Whether you're with a significant other, family members, or friends, or are part of an organized outdoor group, knowing and following a few key principles can help make the process of teaching and learning easier and more enjoyable for everyone.

GUIDELINES FOR TEACHERS

- Before you presume to teach something, you should honestly ask yourself if you have the necessary skills to not only perform the activity but also to teach it to others. At the very least, you should read books about the activity and how to teach it. You should also think carefully about what you're trying to teach and the best ways to teach the individuals with whom you'll be working.
- Think about the needs of your partners, both as your partners and as your students. Understanding the intellectual and physical differences, emotional needs, and other characteristics of students is often far more important to successful teaching than mere technical mastery.
- When teaching partners, remember to consider issues of roles, power, vulnerability, and self-esteem.
- Think about what you are doing as a teacher. Know the reason for your demonstration or instruction and be able to explain the rationale behind it. The best teaching is a combination of strategy, technique, and art. Good teachers fully understand the activity, are able to sense what their students need, and can develop exercises and explanations that enable students to understand and acquire new skills.
- Use many modes of teaching. Some people learn best through verbal instruction, others need visual demonstrations, and others may need kinesthetic experience. To meet the needs of different learners, experienced instructors follow this sequence: (1) Explain the exercise. (2) Demonstrate the exercise. (3) Have students perform the exercise. (4) Provide feedback and repeat steps one through three as needed.

- Be generous and positive in praising accomplishments and progress. As you watch a student perform something, try to always look for what is right as well as what is wrong with his or her technique. Tell students what they're doing well before you offer suggestions for what to do better.

- Do not feel that you always have to make a suggestion for change. Often, just giving praise and letting the person practice more is the best thing you can do.

- Use imagery and metaphor as teaching tools. Finding the correct image is one of the distinguishing features of great teachers.

- A good way to better match your instruction to your students is to think about what other activities—recreational, vocational, or otherwise—that the student does and how elements or concepts from those activities might carry over to the one you're teaching.

- Ask other teachers how they teach and take every opportunity to watch skilled teachers at work. All of us learn what we do from others and there is nothing wrong with copying the ways in which other instructors teach. Even the most experienced professional instructors continue to attend teaching clinics and to sit in on classes taught by their peers.

- If you haven't been explicitly identified as an instructor but think you have useful suggestions to offer, ask permission of your partners before teaching them. Teaching is more likely to be received well if it is wanted to begin with.

- Don't try to teach too many things at once. Even if you see ten things going wrong, pick the one that's likely to produce the most results and focus on that. As a general rule, try to not give more than one suggestion at a time and try to limit yourself to addressing three or four parts of any activity in a given day. If you try to work on more skills all at once, people tend to get confused and overwhelmed. (In this list, I've broken this rule by offering many suggestions. The nature of teaching with a book allows and requires one to put everything down at once. However, in your "real-life" teaching, keep it simple! There will be plenty of time to give more suggestions. Don't try to do it all at once.)

- Give lots of practice on one skill before introducing something new. If you offer a suggestion, let the student try it for a while before introducing another instruction. A good way to determine when to offer a second suggestion or exercise is simply to let the student work with what you have told him or her, then ask the student if he or she is ready to try something new.

- Don't get personally upset if your partner doesn't want to try something. If your partner doesn't want to do something and you find yourself becoming upset, ask yourself what it is that is upsetting your partner and what is upsetting you. Is your partner resisting because of the way you are teaching? Is he or she tired or hurt? Is what appears to be resistance really fear? Are you feeling frustrated because your desires to succeed as an instructor are not being met? Are you expecting something from your partner that is not realistic? Is this situation similar to others in your relationship? What else might be going on?

- Remember that anger almost always interferes with effective learning or teaching. Don't waste your time trying to teach while angry. It almost surely won't work, and even if it did work, it would take the fun out of what you are doing.

- Be patient if things do not come along quickly. Remember, once we learn an activity, we forget what it was like to learn. Keep in mind that people learn different activities at different rates. Don't blame your partner or yourself if things move slowly. Accept that pace and work with it rather than against it.

- Invite feedback about your teaching. Give your partner a chance to tell you what is helping and what isn't. Then, don't try to defend your approach. Just listen fully to what he or she says. By listening to suggestions, you not only learn how to teach better, you also model a positive attitude toward learning.

- Know when to not teach. It may be true that we are constantly learning, but it is not true that every moment is as good as another for teaching or learning with our partners.

- Develop your awareness of factors and situations that are not optimal for teaching. Consider your partner's physical condition, mood, equipment, the weather, and other factors that can block effective teaching and learning.

- Be aware of social pressures that can interfere with learning. In the presence of others, we may feel on the spot as teachers or learners.

- Know when to stop. Learn to recognize when things are going well. Then, instead of going on to teach five more skills, let that be enough teaching for the day.

- Finally, and most importantly, keep things fun. Remember why you are doing the activity and why you're doing it together.

GUIDELINES FOR LEARNERS

- Determine your willingness to learn and to learn from the person who is teaching you. If there is a reason why you don't want to learn from a partner, it's better to not start a process in which you aren't invested.
- Be as clear as you can with yourself and your partner about your goals for the activity. Instructors tend to assume that all students want to become experts, but many students are satisfied with achieving only minimal goals and some don't really care about learning, they simply want to have a good time.
- Ask yourself if you're ready to learn. For all learning, one must be in a proper frame of mind, and for many outdoor activities, one must be prepared physically and with the proper equipment.
- Communicate any special needs or concerns. Students should not expect instructors to read their minds. If you have specific concerns or unique physical needs, or if you're frightened or worried about something, help your instructors help you by telling them from the start.
- Talk with your instructor about how you learn best. If you need visual cues, or if verbal suggestions are valuable, or if you like to do a lot of observation, let your instructor know.
- Be willing to try new things even though they may sound, look, or feel strange at first. Few things are more frustrating to instructors than students who say they want to learn but then are unwilling to try anything new.
- Tell your partner if a specific suggestion or teaching approach helps or if a suggestion or approach is not working for you. Instructors need feedback just as much as students.
- Be patient with yourself and your partner if things don't come to you quickly. Learning takes time and everyone learns different things at different rates.
- Don't worry about comparing yourself to other students. Do your best, work at your own pace, and focus on the successes along the way.
- Recognize when you need time to practice without new suggestions

or when you have had enough for the day. If you become aware that you're getting overloaded, gently let your partner know you've had enough instruction for the day.

▪ Finally, the most important guideline is to keep things fun. Remember why you're learning the activity and why you're doing it together.

PROFESSIONAL INSTRUCTION

One final note about learning outdoor activities: Although the guidelines offered above for teachers and learners should help partners be more successful, many times the best way to learn and to prevent relationship accidents is by taking lessons from a professional. With a professional instructor, one is free to focus on learning without having to please, impress, or worry about the relationship with one's partner. Meanwhile, more experienced partners can do more challenging activities without feeling they have to teach, wait, or otherwise hold back. Thus, each person is getting something he or she needs without putting strain on the relationship. After the lessons, partners can get together just to enjoy the activity, not to learn from or teach each other.

CHAPTER 9

MEN AND WOMEN:
DEALING WITH STEREOTYPES AND WORKING WITH DIFFERENCES

"I can't figure out if we're supposed to treat each other like we're completely equal in everything, or if it's okay to have some differences. It's really confusing sometimes."

"I heard this guy below say, 'She climbs pretty good for a girl.' I just wanted to drop the biggest rock I could find smack onto him."

THROUGHOUT THIS BOOK THE FOCUS has been on relationships between people, regardless of gender. There are two reasons for this. First, I wanted to avoid stereotypes about men, women, and the outdoors. Second, experience has shown time and again that differences between people of the same gender are often much larger than differences between people of different genders.

While trying to avoid stereotypes is important, it would also be foolish to ignore the equally important fact that in our society there *are* differences between how men and women are raised to act, feel, think, and communicate with members of their own sex and with members of the opposite sex. There are also critical differences between what men and women are taught in regard to their relationships with one another and with the outdoors.

This chapter offers insights that may help men and women better understand themselves and relate to each other in the outdoors. The challenge is to facilitate understanding without creating new stereotypes that unfairly categorize people. Thus, keep in mind that there are always individual exceptions to any general statements. I also want to emphasize that speaking about relationships between men and women is not in any way intended to limit the discussion of this book to heterosexual relationships. While the next section emphasizes male-female relationships, many of the concepts are equally useful to same-sex couples.

STEREOTYPES ABOUT GENDERS AND THE OUTDOORS

Like it or not, gender stereotypes have a significant influence on outdoor relationships. One way to demonstrate this would be to randomly select a group of people and ask them to put the word *male* or *female* beside each adjective in the list below. Which adjectives would be designated male and which female by the majority of the population?

Wilderness	Home
Climber	Shopper
Courageous	Frightened
Independent	Dependent
Tough	Weak

Of course, we don't actually have to conduct a survey to know which genders would be associated with which adjectives. Clearly, men and women have to deal with much different messages about themselves and about one another in the outdoors. Those messages are so pervasive and powerful that they simply must affect outdoor relationships and in most instances do so adversely.

As long as society explicitly and implicitly teaches males and females that they are expected to feel and act differently in relation to outdoor activities, those expectations will affect our relationships in countless ways that we may not be aware of. What happens, for example, if a man has less outdoor experiences or knowledge than a woman? Or if a woman wants to be more involved in the outdoors but her friends or family don't feel it would be "ladylike"? If we conform to stereotypes, our options to think or act in different ways are limited. But if we do not conform, we must deal with the social pressure to fit in.

PHYSICAL APPEARANCE

Apart from images that directly relate to outdoor activities, other male-female images also affect our outdoor relationships. This was discovered by a couple who argued about what a person should bring along on a camping trip. While looking for something in his partner's pack, Carl was surprised to find a very small makeup kit. Although the kit actually weighed just a few ounces and took less space than a small flashlight, Carl took it out and, in front of their hiking companions, made great fun of the fact that his partner Karen had brought along a lipstick and small tube of face cream. "Maybe there's an evening gown in there too," he laughed, "just in case we get invited to a formal occasion. Rats, and I forgot my tux."

As if this wasn't enough, the teasing was followed by a lecture on traveling light and not bringing unnecessary extras that weigh you down. Karen didn't find Carl's antics amusing, but the barbs and lecture stung and left her feeling humiliated. As she talked about the experience later, Karen explained that she was well aware of the need to save weight and space, but her decision to bring the lipstick was a response to other concerns. "It's easy for men to criticize women for bringing things like makeup along on trips," she said, "but men don't have to worry about their appearance in the same way women do."

Women in our society are indoctrinated from childhood on the importance of looking attractive. Even the outdor magazines that put women on their covers always choose women that are exceptionally attractive and often wearing only boots, shorts, halter tops, and fetching smiles—and most likely makeup. What's more, while men may ridicule their partners for bringing makeup on a trip, those same men are likely to make comments about how attractive certain other women are. Whether or not they realize it, in making such comments men are emphasizing the need for the very appurtenances for which they have criticized their partners.

Karen said it well: "We're in a no-win situation. Guys tell us it's silly to care about how we look when we're camping, but then they go on and on about how other women look. Even if they say they don't care, men pay more attention to women who look a certain way. With all these messages, you can't help but think it matters how you look wherever you are."

Both men and women have roles to play in changing this. Women can stand their ground and insist that they should not have to be any more concerned than men about physical appearances in the outdoors. They can also break out of the commercial images of what constitutes "beauty" or "attractiveness" and begin to feel comfortable with how they look as they are, rather than as magazines would have them look in order to sell products.

"I'm not hiking because I want someone to look at me and think I'm beautiful," said one woman hiker. "I'm doing it because I think nature is beautiful. I refuse to believe I have to wear nylons, heels, and lipstick and have my hair done in order to be accepted or respected as a person. Half the reason for getting outdoors in the first place is to get away from all that nonsense."

Another woman described how repeated sexist remarks and the underlying attitude of a male guide ruined what otherwise would have been a wonderful experience. "We had come to learn how to climb, but instead we had to put up with this guy's crude remarks about women being weaker. He was also full of sexual innuendos that made all of us uncomfortable. I thought we were past that, but I guess there are still a lot of jerks left who haven't caught on."

For their part, men need to become more aware of double standards and the binds in which women are placed. Snide comments about women's appearances, sexist remarks about their bodies or clothing, ogling other women, and other such actions serve to insult women in general and as individuals. Many men insist they "don't mean anything" by their comments, or women should "not be so sensitive." But the real problem is the action of the men, not the reaction of the women.

Fortunately, many men have made real changes. More and more men are escaping the stereotypical images of physical beauty and are coming to understand the experiences of women in our society. Beyond simply avoid sexist actions themselves, they are actively challenging those of others and supporting women who are working for change.

THE "STRONGER SEX"

While women are influenced by physical appearance issues, men are also trapped by stereotypes, but in different ways. The notion of males as the "stronger sex" creates an image that men often feel they have to live up to in the outdoors. Even if a man has never done an outdoor activity before, there is an expectation that, simply because he is a man, he will like whatever the activity is, will know how to do it, and will be good at it. If these expectations are not met, a man just isn't considered a man.

It's as if we assume that somewhere wound up in the Y chromosome there are instructions that say every man will love the outdoors and will know how to climb mountains, build fires, wrestle bears, fix flats, etc. For many men, this expectation makes it hard to try new activities for fear of looking foolish. It also makes it hard for men to accept women who are more capable in the outdoors. Communication with partners is also affected because "strong men" aren't supposed to talk about their feelings or let anyone know if they're in pain and need a break.

Much as women are seeking to get beyond traditional gender stereotypes, many men are challenging the assumption that they have to be strong and accomplished in everything they try or in all outdoor activities. They recognize that such assumptions are ludicrous and can only interfere with their enjoyment and their relationships.

"I used to take charge of everything and assume my way was always right" said one man. "But my wife has set me straight. Now we discuss things together before making decisions, and I really respect her opinions. Lots of times she sees things differently and her ideas turn out to work better than mine would have. That's not how my parents did it, but they probably would have been a lot happier if they had."

Another man spoke of how he once felt he had to do all of the "dirty work," like cleaning equipment, preparing the car, etc. He sometimes resented this but never thought to include his partner. When she asked one day if she could help, he was at first surprised but then thought about it and welcomed her involvement. Now they perform these tasks jointly, considering them as one more way in which they can share all aspects of their outdoor pursuits.

NEW TRAPS IN RESISTING STEREOTYPES

Along with the pressure to conform to traditional gender models, there's also the reverse risk that people will try so hard to *not* be anything like the traditional model that they aren't free to feel or express certain emotions or behaviors that might actually be good for them and their partners. There may also be a tendency to deny that any differences of any kind exist between men and women. These are understandable reactions to the sexism of the past, but trying to not be anything like a stereotype can become just as limiting as trying rigidly to conform.

One couple, Brandon and June, described a heated late-night argument that took place the third night of a week-long canoe trip. At the end of a long day of paddling into the wind, both were very tired and the mood seemed unusually heavy as they ate. To lighten the air, June made a joke about Brandon's cooking of the evening's macaroni and cheese dinner. "Have you ever heard of something called salt?" she asked. Much to her surprise, Brandon took the plate from her hands and dumped all the food into the campfire.

In the course of the exchange that followed, it turned out that Brandon was sensitive about his cooking and was also feeling that he was doing more than his share of it during their trip. For her part, June wanted to do more of the cooking but she hadn't said anything because Brandon had taken control of cooking without asking for her input. With the gates open, other matters were now raised. June complained that Brandon left her in the back of the canoe most of the time and she couldn't see as well from there. Brandon countered that he did that because the back is where the control is and he didn't want to be sexist and take that from her just because he was a man. In fact, he would have been happy to spend more time in back because he too liked guiding. Next on the list were issues about who planned the trip, who read the maps, who made decisions, etc. Finally, June complained that sometimes she just wanted Brandon to hold her and to feel comforted by his strength. Brandon acknowledged that sometimes he wanted to be taken care of too, but he never felt he could ask that lest he leave June with the traditional "women's" work.

Through this discussion, Brandon and June realized they were both making such an effort to not fill the typical male and female roles that they were not doing things they needed or wanted to do for themselves and each other. This discovery led to an agreement: instead of trying to fill or to not fill fixed roles, and instead of assuming they knew what their partner did or did not want, they would talk about what was happening and what they needed. They also agreed to not let things build up as they had prior to their argument about the macaroni.

After relating the argument and its resolution, June laughed and said, "Then we went into the tent and made love." She added, however, that once in their sleeping bags, they realized they were still trying so hard to not fit stereotypes that they were not really as free or open as they wanted to be. They talked about this and agreed to communicate better about their needs and desires. June described the results by saying, "We didn't get much sleep that night, but it wasn't because we were fighting."

DIFFERENCES IN COMMUNICATION STYLES

One of the reasons partners experience communication problems is that most of us are not consciously aware of our own communication patterns or how we developed them. We also have little awareness of how our communication style affects our partner or that there could be any alternative to the way we have always done things. This is particularly relevant to gender issues because men and women are socialized to communicate in different ways.

To illustrate how communication differences can affect interactions between men and women, consider the dialogues below. Assume that the person identified as L is a woman. What do you think is the gender of J in each example?

> L: *"I'm cold."*
> J: *"Why don't you zip up your jacket and put a hat on?"*

Version two of the same interaction:

> L: *"I'm cold."*
> J: *"Me too. It's really chilly tonight."*

Even though this is a very brief exchange, most people guess that J is probably a male in the first example but is probably a female in the second. This tells a lot about how men and women communicate with each other. In general, men tend to respond to communication as pieces of information to be processed for the purpose of finding solutions or exchanging other information. This has to do both with communication styles and with how men see their role in relationship to women in outdoor activities. Men tend to think of themselves as problem solvers and they often assume (consciously or unconsciously) that women could not solve problems themselves if the men were not around.

By comparison, women tend to respond more to the emotional content of communications and are typically attuned to what is happening interpersonally at least as much as what is happening in the activity. This is also connected to how women see their role in relationships and in the outdoors. Instead of offering solutions to a partner's problems, women are more likely to empathize and share the problem in some way. When a woman says she is cold, she is more likely to be simply expressing a feeling than seeking advice on how to stay warm.

Conflicts tend to arise in relationships when communications are crossed. If one person expects a certain kind of response from a partner but receives a much different reply, that person is likely to feel frustrated. At the same time, if someone is sincerely trying to help a partner but the help seems unappreciated, that person is likely to feel frustrated.

In addition to recognizing how conflicts can stem from crossed communications, we should also be aware that gender stereotypes can add to such problems. If we consider the first interaction between J and L in the context of social roles, we see how in just a two-sentence interaction many of the social role models are played out. Let's assume for the moment that L is a woman and J is a man. By mentioning that she is cold, L made herself vulnerable, only to receive instructions in return. J, on the other hand, tried to respond helpfully by offering suggestions, but because suggestions were not really what L was looking for, J's response may not be appreciated. As a result, he too is likely to be frustrated but for different reasons.

It's important to understand that this type of interaction is by no means limited to partners who feel there are major problems in their relationships. Indeed, such dialogues are perhaps typical of most relationships. The point is not to identify a single interaction pattern and say it is the source of all problems or is found in all couples. What matters is awareness of the importance of communication styles and the appreciation that it is worth your trouble to think and talk with each other about the communication patterns in your own relationship. If problems in communication seem to be a recurrent part of your relationship, try to work with your partners to get past whose way is "right" or "wrong." Then you can begin to understand what differences may exist that you haven't recognized before and how those differences are affecting your interactions. More is said about communications in chapter 10, Communication for Outdoor Partners.

DIFFERENCES IN PHYSICAL ABILITIES

On average, people with greater muscle mass are physically stronger than people with less muscle mass. Because men—again, on average—have greater muscle mass than women, in general men are also physically stronger than women. This does not mean there are not plenty of women who are far stronger than plenty of men, and it refers solely to physical strength, not stamina, which is far more dependent on training and attitude than gender alone. It does, however, mean that for most mixed-gender partners who do outdoor sports, men are able to lift and carry more than women.

The reason for starting this discussion by speaking about *muscle mass* and strength rather than *gender* and strength is that if people are to take into account strength as a factor in their outdoor activities, they need to do just that: consider strength, not gender. This does not mean one person is bad and the other good. It simply means one person has more of a certain capability that is needed to perform certain things. If that is the reality, what is the problem?

The problem is, reality is not so simple. In outdoor relationships, matters of physical differences are closely tied to other issues, such as our assumptions about what qualities are valued in people and who has power in relationships. To appreciate this, we need only consider the two adjectives we use to describe physical ability: stronger and weaker. These are not mere words used to describe physical condition. In our society, to be strong is considered good, while to be weak is scorned. Because of the values that strength and weakness carry with them, physical differences between people imply far more than the mere fact of who can lift more weight.

Two friends who did a lot of hiking together described that for their first backpacking trip together, the woman insisted that she carry no less weight in her pack than the man had in his. The man, Robert, was about six feet two inches tall and weighed around 190 pounds. The woman, Carol, was five feet three and weighed about 110 pounds. Robert offered to carry the bulk of the load, but Carol insisted that she have an equal amount of weight. They divided the material equally, leaving each with what they later estimated to be at least 60 pounds to carry on their first day of a five-day trip through rather rugged and steep terrain. A 60-pound pack is pretty brutal no matter how strong one is, but a quick calculation of the ratio of pack to body weight reveals that Carol was carrying more than half her own body weight, while Robert was carrying slightly more than a third of his. In spite of this, Carol adamantly refused to carry any less. The result was that the hike went much more slowly than planned and, although she was able to make it, Carol was thoroughly exhausted and in significant discomfort at the end of each day.

When some people hear of Carol's attitude, they are critical of her for not being "rational" or for "trying to prove something." Carol, however, explained that she had given a lot of thought to the matter and had good reasons for what she was doing. She pointed out that the phrase "can't carry their load" is derogatory whenever it is used, but it is often directed at women. "It may be fine to talk in the abstract about carrying equal proportions of body weight," she said, "but I don't want my partners thinking I don't have as much real weight to carry as they do." Carol also explained that she didn't want to be in any way indebted to a man because he carried more weight than her. It was important for her to know she could be independent, and if she had to count on someone else to carry things for her, she would be depending on him. "It would be like I couldn't make the trip without having someone else there. That isn't true and I don't want to give anyone an excuse to think it is."

Finally, Carol added, "You know, it's really unfair. If a woman doesn't carry as much weight as a man, she feels dependent and is put down for being weak. If she does carry as much, she gets insulted for trying to prove something or for being 'irrational.' What I would really like is to cut through all that crap and get to where we can go out to have fun together without judging each other at all. Then, maybe, I'd be willing to go by percentage of body weight or something and let someone else carry more than me. Maybe."

Different but equally challenging issues are raised in situations where women are more physically capable than their male partners.

Peter and Eva, a couple in their mid-thirties, described how difficulties arose in their relationship when they began to participate in fun runs and discovered that Eva could run faster than Peter. As they ran in more races, Eva began to place among the top women runners and finished several minutes ahead of Peter. Describing his reactions, Peter explained that he found himself experiencing a combination of pride and jealousy about Eva's accomplishments. "I was happy for her that she was doing so well, but at the same time it wasn't easy for me to be left struggling behind while she charged ahead and made it look so easy." Peter continued, "It was really hard when friends asked about our running and made jokes about how could I 'let my wife beat me.' There wasn't any 'let' about it," Peter said. "Eva was just better than I was and I had to get used to it."

CREATIVE SOLUTIONS TO PHYSICAL DIFFERENCES

If couples are to deal with physical differences constructively, the first step is to return to the question asked in chapter 6: "What are we doing this for?"

If we pursue outdoor activities as tests of personal strength or to prove our superiority over others, it's probably going to be difficult to supportively adjust to our partner's differences in physical strength or abilities. On the other hand, if the goal of outdoor activities together is to have fun and build the strength of the relationship, partners are more likely to think in terms of their mutual goals, abilities, and accomplishments as a team. Therefore, an essential part of learning to deal with physical differences is for partners to ask themselves and each other why they're doing the activity to begin with, and why they want to do it together.

In another example of carrying weight backpacking, a couple who successfully resolved strength differences took a trial-and-error approach in which they began by dividing loads according to body weight. From there, experience showed that one partner could comfortably carry a greater proportion of the weight, so she gradually took more in her pack. This process was further aided by their discovery of ways to save on their overall loads by taking fewer and lighter things.

A somewhat different solution was achieved by a couple in which one was a more dedicated and fit cyclist than his partner. When they went cycling together, they typically rode for a number of miles side by side, then the stronger cyclist rode ahead several miles and returned, meeting his partner and joining him again for the next several miles. Another strategy for them was for one to ride in front at a fast pace while the other drafted behind. Whichever approach they used, both were able to enjoy the ride without feeling like one was pushed "too hard" or the other was held back.

Yet another couple solved the problem of strength differences by purchasing a double sea kayak. With the double kayak, when one person got tired and the other still felt strong, the one could rest while the other continued paddling.

The ways people deal with physical differences may vary, but the key to successful resolution is the same: the desire and willingness of each partner to find ways they can both have fun together. With mutual enjoyment as the top priority, and good communication between them, partners who work together don't get hung up on trying to prove anything or on becoming obsessively concerned that everything is exactly equal. Instead, they find what works for each person individually and for the partnership as a team.

DIFFERENCES IN ANATOMY

Another area of undeniable physical differences between the sexes has to do with male and female anatomy and physiological functioning. Such matters as "going to the bathroom" where there is no bathroom, personal cleanliness, menstrual cycles, etc., all pose challenges in the outdoors that are obviously different for men than women but are often not well understood or dealt with by partners.

HUMAN WASTES

The brilliant psychoanalyst Karen Horney once challenged Sigmund Freud's infamous notion of penis envy and argued that, if anything, men should be jealous of women who, after all, are endowed with responsibility and power for the greatest miracle of all, childbirth. If women envy the penis at all, argued Horney, it is because in our society the people with penises have all the social power and keep women from getting any because they are so jealous of what women can do that they cannot. Hence, Horney asserted, penis envy should really be reframed as power envy.

With respect and apologies to Dr. Horney, there is perhaps one small additional reason for penis envy. Again, this benefit is minuscule in comparison to the responsibility and power of childbirth, but there is little denying that when it comes to relieving one's bladder in the wilderness, the penis is a handy thing to have. For that matter, it's not a bad deal to be possessed of a bit larger bladder so one has to take care of such business less frequently.

A woman climber I know acknowledges that there may in fact be certain advantages to male anatomy when the wind chill is minus twenty degrees, and climbing harnesses and pants are cinched tight. "But why," she asks, "does that particular piece of hardware so often come with such small brains that seem incapable of understanding? It's easy for a man to say, 'Don't be silly, just go.' He doesn't have to bare his buns to the wind or to whoever else might come strolling by. I've gotten used to the business by now," she said, "but I have sure climbed with some juvenile partners."

This woman's point was echoed by many women. It isn't simply the added hassle that bothers them, it's the failure of men to understand that hassle. "A little sensitivity would help a lot," said one.

In case sensitivity is hard to come by, there are also some technical fixes that can ease the problem. Recently, a woman hiker came out with a line of pants with specially designed flaps for women. Another option is the disposable paper funnel, which some women swear by. For relief inside a tent on freezing nights, my wife and I have found that a large food storage bag with a zip-locking top serves as a handy porta-potty for men and women alike. This literally saved our bladders one night while camped on a glacier in a screaming wind. Since that night, we always carry a few such bags as standard equipment.

Men and women are on more equal footing with regard to defecation. Here, I confess, I don't know of any magical technical solutions (perhaps NASA has some suggestions), but a bit of understanding is much appreciated. For practical and humorous pointers about how to do your business in an environmentally correct way, check out *How to Shit in the Woods: An Environmentally Sound Approach to a Lost Art* (Ten Speed Press, 1994). Another good resource is *Wilderness Basics: The Complete Handbook for Hikers and Backpackers* (The Mountaineers, 1993).

Several couples admitted that when they first began hiking they were quite modest about the whole issue of elimination. Eventually, however, nature created situations in which such modesty had to give way to necessity. For example, the woman climber mentioned earlier often asks her husband to provide at least a modicum of shelter by standing nearby to obscure the view of others. Other partners sometimes serve as lookouts, and one man said he sometimes acts as a diversion. When his partner is off to one side of a trail taking care of business, if he sees other hikers approaching, he begins to look intently and excitedly into the woods on the opposite side of the trail. As the strangers approach he motions them to look, and for added effect he holds a finger to his lips as if to suggest that quiet is important. When everyone is near enough, he explains that he thought he saw a bear or some other creature. This ruse goes on as long as it takes for his partner to finish and join him. Then with a wink at one another, he says, "Hmm, well, maybe it wasn't a bear," and they continue on.

Remember that if human waste is disposed of, it should be done well away from campsites and trails and at least 200 feet from water sources; toilet paper should be packed out, not buried or burned. In high-use areas, such as popular trails and frequently climbed mountains, the best practice is to pack out all waste. This is not necessarily the most pleasant task, but with more and more people in the outdoors, we simply must keep our natural places from turning into vast toilets. One way to do this is to bring along sealable plastic bags into which the waste, toilet paper, and other material can be placed. Some campers also bring along small sealable hard-plastic containers in which they pack out the waste-filled bags for further protection.

MENSTRUAL CYCLES

No matter how well they may try to plan ahead, many women have had the unpleasant surprise of a period starting when they are miles from nowhere with no tampons or sanitary pads to be found. One solution for this is to include a few tampons and sanitary pads as a regular part of one's first-aid kit, then always be sure to bring the kit along. In addition to serving their intended function, sanitary napkins are good to have in a first-aid kit because they are well suited as dressings for large wounds.

Personal hygiene is another issue that is different for women than men and that becomes particularly important during menstrual periods. Experienced women hikers often bring along a small washcloth, soap, and a small towel that they use to stay clean along the trail. This can be easily and compactly carried in a sealable plastic bag. This added weight and space may provide one more source of complaint or criticism from male companions but, once again, women may need to set them straight and men need to understand the issues.

For many women, menstrual cramps can be extraordinarily painful and even disabling. Partners who hike with women should be aware of and sensitive to this fact and should be willing to make accommodations. Again, it is easy for a man to say, "Okay, I know it's unpleasant, but it can't hurt that bad. You could come with us if you really wanted to." Men do not have to deal with the pain, so they cannot really know what the woman is experiencing. If they really care about and respect their partner, they will not add to what is already an unpleasant experience.

If painful cramps are common to a woman, she and her partners may need to plan their outings with that fact in mind. Some women simply choose to stay home during their period. This may sound like an inconvenience, and to some extent it is, but one woman said, "My partner and I are out probably three weekends out of four in the summer. Staying home once a month really isn't so bad. Besides, I've tried toughing it out before and it just isn't worth it."

Others continue to go out but have contingency plans: If the pain is too severe they may not hike as far, or perhaps they will simply spend the day reading in camp. Still others are able to manage their symptoms through medications. Once again, there is no "right" or "wrong" way to deal with this. What matters most is that partners communicate with one another and adapt their plans to take into account each person's needs.

One final topic to address in regard to periods has to do with the danger of bears or other animals. During their periods, women are advised to not venture into bear country. It is thought that the scent of blood may incite the bears and possibly provoke an attack. Partners are also advised to abstain from sexual behavior in bear country, again out of concern that scents could trigger a response from bears.

If a period does start when one is in the backcountry, be particularly careful about disposing of tampons or sanitary pads. These should be carried out like other solid waste, but be careful to follow the kinds of procedures practiced to protect food from animals. Use sealable plastic bags to keep waste separate and reduce odors. When in camp, hang these bags from trees or place them in other safe locations that would not attract curious or hungry animals into your tent.

DIFFERENCES IN RISK FROM HUMAN DANGERS

The risks from the most dangerous animal in the outdoors—humans—is raised here because it is especially pertinent to the issue of differences between the sexes.

HUMAN DANGERS FOR WOMEN

A fundamental fact of existence that few men fully appreciate but women can deny only at their peril is that women who are alone face certain risks from men that men who are alone much less commonly have to concern themselves with. If a man wants to go hiking on a trail alone, he has the chance to enjoy the solitude of nature, experience some time to himself, and perhaps get away from some of the troubles of the civilized world. The primary fears a man has to deal with are the normal risks of nature and of simply being alone.

The world is much different for women. In addition to any other hazards of nature, women must consider the possibility of being raped and murdered. If a woman does hike alone and is assaulted, she faces the very real likelihood that people will blame her for having had the temerity to do something men can do without a second thought.

Near my home is a short nature trail that I often take at the end of training runs. No matter how friendly and non-threatening I might try to be, when I encounter women walking alone on the trail I can almost sense their fear. For a woman alone on the trail, the peace is obviously disrupted by the awareness that a stranger is present and there might be a risk of assault. This is a terrible reality, but our society continues to tolerate it, women have to live with it, and most men simply do not understand what that is like.

In outdoor relationships, this issue can arise in a variety of ways. For example, if a couple or members of a group become separated, it is a much different matter for a woman than for a man to walk on a trail alone, or wait for others at a trailhead or parking lot. Car camping is also far different. I recently spoke with a group of women who were having a wonderful time camped near a river until a pickup truck full of rowdy young men drove past and did the predictable whistles and yells. For the rest of the evening and into the night, the women feared the men might return with an intent to harm them.

This issue is further heightened by the fact that in most situations, there are fewer women present in the outdoors than men. On a very hot hike with a group of friends, we came upon a lake and several of the men stripped and jumped in for a refreshing dip. The one woman along was reluctant to join and the men could not understand why. What they failed to appreciate was that there were two other groups of hikers present, all of whom were males. This made the woman the only female among about a dozen males, many of whom she did not know.

"The guys had absolutely no idea what that was like for me," she said later. "Of course I wanted to go swimming and I would have loved to be naked. But not with all those men around, especially the ones I didn't know. At the very least they would be watching me and I would feel awkward. But on top of that, I was frightened. Not that my friends would have let anything happen, but it's really uncomfortable anyway to be the only woman, and it is just too much to be the only woman and be undressed too. I had to just wade and splash water on myself and put up with some really juvenile comments. One more 'fun adventure' with guys."

HUMAN DANGERS FOR MEN

While emphasizing the unique dangers faced by women, it should not be forgotten that men also face dangers from others. Sexual assaults are less common against males, but they do happen, especially against young males. Of much greater frequency among adult men are violent confrontations that often arise over trivial matters.

A friend who bicycles tells of an incident in which a car passed him too closely and he responded with a vertical hand signal that did not mean "left turn." The car screeched to a halt and several men got out and began running toward the cyclist. He was able to turn just in time and ride away, but then the car also turned and pursued him. Fortunately, a police car happened by and he was able to get assistance. "Had it not been for that," my friend said later, "I think those guys probably would have killed me."

However frightening the car passing too closely may have been, and however much those of us who cycle can understand the desire to respond in some way, provoking such a dangerous reaction from the driver was not a good idea. "The kind of guy who passes you like that in the first place may be the kind of guy who will come back and get you if you flip him off. I'm just lucky he didn't have a gun," concluded my friend.

Another man described an altercation he was involved in with a climber who refused to stop smoking a cigarette on top of a mountain summit. Strong words were exchanged and it looked like a fight was imminent, but cooler friends prevailed and separated the two.

What is remarkable about these events is that serious physical harm could easily have happened for no good reason. Something about the way many men are raised and socialized makes them respond with anger and the threat of violence to even minor affronts. This is dangerous not only to the men involved, it can also threaten their partners. A woman told of a harrowing high-speed car chase in which her husband adamantly refused to quit pursuing another car that he felt had cut him off while passing. This happened while on the way to a vacation at a mountain lake where they were going for some "peace and quiet."

Recognizing his own potential for such actions, and having narrowly averted several dangerous altercations, at least one man said he finally realized he had to make some changes. "I was really angry," he said, "and I was always ready to get into it with someone. But one day I realized that I could actually get killed or maybe even kill someone else for nothing. I started asking myself if it's worth it to flip someone off, or swear at 'em or whatever else I used to do. Now, no matter how angry I get, I stop first and ask myself, 'Is this worth a life?' The answer is always 'No.' Now what I'm working on," he continued, "is understanding where all that anger came from in the first place."

FINDING PEACE IN NATURE AND WITHIN OURSELVES

Violence is part of our society, but we do not have to accept violence as a natural or permanent condition. It is intolerable that women cannot enjoy the same freedom of mind and body as men do, whether it is in the outdoors or in a city. And it is a tragic statement about our nation and society that violence is a leading cause of death among young men. These conditions simply must be changed and it is up to each of us to play a part in that process.

As men and women, we can begin to bring about change by working together to understand our own experiences and those of our partners and by supporting one another as we seek to cope with conditions as they are today. We can also be an active part of efforts to help people resolve differences in ways that are constructive rather than destructive. If we go to the outdoors to find peace, we can bring that peace back to help us make personal changes and to help our society as a whole become safe for everyone.

CHAPTER 10

COMMUNICATION FOR OUTDOOR PARTNERS

"Let me kayak class V, climb 5.11, or run a marathon, but don't ask me to talk about how I'm feeling."

"You want to know how my partner and I communicate? Let's just say that if we don't have anything nice to say, we don't say anything, so most of the time it's pretty quiet."

WHEN PEOPLE ARE ASKED TO NAME the single most important thing they could do to improve their outdoor relationships, the most common answer is "better communication." Partners who are having relationship problems almost universally express that if they could just communicate better, most of their problems would be solved.

Although it isn't possible in a few short pages to provide solutions for all of the communication problems that can affect relationships, there are some basic skills that are relatively easy to learn and that can help us through many of the situations that outdoor partners face. If you review the conflicts you've experienced in relationships, you will probably discover that many could have been prevented or more successfully resolved if you or your partner had followed the principles listed below.

COMMUNICATION BASICS

- Meet your partners where they are at the moment. At any point during a communication, even in the middle of heated arguments, you can begin to work toward a constructive result by showing that you genuinely want to understand what your partners are saying or feeling.
- Start by trying to understand your partners. Rather than focusing on how you think your partners need to change, work instead on how you can better understand their experience from their perspective, not yours.
- Listen. Try to listen to what your partners are communicating—both verbally and nonverbally. Don't assume you know what someone is thinking or feeling. If you don't know what your partner is experiencing, ask.
- Talk. If you do not talk with your partners, do not expect them to know what you are thinking or feeling or what you need. When you do talk, tell what you are experiencing personally, not what you think is "wrong" with your partner.
- Pay attention to the process of your interactions. Try to focus more on *how* things are said rather than simply what is said. In other words, keep in mind the process of your communications as well as the content of what is being communicated.
- Be willing to call a time-out. There may be circumstances when conflict has arisen and you will need to take a break in order to get something essential accomplished or to give one another time to

reflect and settle down. If practical circumstances or your emotional state do not allow for constructive communication, let some time pass until you can deal with an issue in a caring, productive way.

■ While outdoors, stay together. No matter how bad communications get, in the outdoors partners must stay together. You can find ways of dealing with things after you're home, but do not let anger, hurt feelings, or other emotions cause you to separate when to do so could be dangerous.

MEETING PEOPLE WHERE THEY ARE

The first rule of effective communication is to meet people where they are by acknowledging and trying to understand their needs and feelings. Until people feel heard and understood, other efforts to resolve conflicts are likely to be ineffective and may well backfire.

Unfortunately, when conflicts arise this principle is rarely followed because people become focused on what they want or feel and how they think their partners should be different. For example, if a person is frightened and seems about to cry, his or her partner might be very likely to say something like, "Don't cry, it's okay." Or if someone is angry and shouting, a partner might say, "Stop shouting and calm down." Such exchanges are so typical that it might be hard to recognize anything lacking in them, but in neither case does the second person's response acknowledge what the first person was feeling. Instead, for what may well be good intentions, both responses tell the person to do or feel something else.

Rather than starting with how we want our partners to change, a more successful approach is to begin by acknowledging that whatever we may think, our partners' behaviors must in some way make sense and have meaning to them. If we can start by trying to understand our partners' perspective, and if we can communicate to them that we sincerely want to understand what they are experiencing, the communication process and eventual outcome are much more likely to be positive.

To revisit the above examples, instead of telling partners who seem frightened or hurt to not cry, a more effective response is to acknowledge that they look like they are hurt, or sad, or are about to cry. This can be followed by a pause to allow them to express whatever they are feeling or need. Similarly, if people are obviously angry, rather than telling them to not be angry or trying immediately to do something to diminish their anger, one is likely to have more success by simply acknowledging their anger, and then, again, allowing them to express what they are feeling. The same approach applies to a variety of situations and feelings.

LISTEN

Listening well is not easy and most of us listen very poorly. That's probably why breakdowns in listening are the trigger points for countless relationship accidents. To illustrate the kinds of listening breakdowns that happen in the outdoors, consider the following exchanges:

> *"I think we should probably take the trail to the right."*
> *"I think it's the trail to the left."*
>
> *"I don't like the looks of that."*
> *"Oh, c'mon, there's nothing to be scared of."*
>
> *"I don't really want to go."*
> *"Sure you do, it'll be fun."*
>
> *"We have to be there by 7."*
> *"Well, there's nothing I can do to be ready by then."*
>
> *"Let's invite Karen and Alex to go with us next weekend."*
> *"I'd prefer to go just by ourselves."*
>
> *"How about . . ."*
> *(interrupting) "I'm sure the pole goes in this sleeve. Grab the other end."*

Some of these exchanges may sound strikingly familiar, and, apart from the interruption in the final example, it might not be apparent that the people involved are not listening. In fact, if those people were asked, they would undoubtedly respond something like, "Of course I was listening. He/she just said . . . then I said . . ."

The fact that we can repeat verbatim what someone has just said means our immediate memory is working, but that is not the same as listening. Notice that in none of the exchanges in these examples does the "listener's" response really acknowledge what the first person said.

Instead of saying, "I listened carefully to what you said and tried to understand," it would be more accurate if the second person said, "I waited for you to finish talking, then I told you what I was thinking."

Rather than interrupting or stating our own position the instant our partners stop speaking, our communications and relationships go better when we show we are interested in and care about what they are saying and what thoughts or feelings are connected to their words. Examples of responses that demonstrate we are really listening include:

> *"I'm not sure I understand what you mean; can you explain it for me?"*

> *"It sounds like your feelings have been hurt."*

> *"Let me think about what you just said for a minute."*

> *"That's interesting because it's different from what I had in mind. From what you're saying, it sounds like you think we should . . ."*

> *"I've got some different ideas about that, but let me hear more about yours and then we can talk about mine and see what we come up with."*

> *"Thanks for telling me you're tired. What would you like to do?"*

The central element of these replies is that they respond to what the speaker has said or is feeling, not primarily to what the listener was thinking. For many people, this type of response probably feels a bit unfamiliar. There may also be good reasons for doing things differently at times, and it may be that many partners are able to communicate just fine without using this method. But it is also possible that partners think they are communicating when they are really just talking and hearing. If that is happening, conflicts are more likely to develop and will be more difficult to resolve.

"LISTENING" TO WHAT ISN'T SAID

Along with listening better to what our partners verbalize, we can further improve relationships by "listening" more attentively to nonverbal messages. For example, if someone is favoring one foot as she or he walks, attentive, receptive partners do not need to wait for that person to say something is wrong. The partner will notice the change in walking and convey that awareness so something can be done to help. Other non-verbal messages while hiking might include frequent adjustments to packstraps, changes in perspiration, slipping or stumbling more on a trail, etc.

A useful way to think about being sensitive to such signals is to consider how experienced outdoorspeople develop their awareness and sensitivity to the natural world. Naturalists, guides, and others who live and work in the outdoors are able to see, hear, smell, and feel things that completely escape the awareness of others.

An experienced and highly regarded outdoor guide told me she tries to use similar awareness and sensitivity when working with her clients on nature trips. "Because people might not tell me everything I need to know," she said, "I have to keep track of what's happening in other ways. I have lots of ways to do that. When we're walking, I listen closely to how people are breathing so I can set the right pace. When we're stopped, I watch for how people take their packs off, how they sit, what they're eating or drinking. What I'm really doing is watching or listening for changes from what people are usually like. When I notice certain changes, that gives me a clue that something might be going on. Most of the time if I just pay attention I can figure out what's up and do something to take care of it without even having to talk to the person."

TALK

Just as hearing the words someone is saying does not mean we are really listening and trying to understand, it's possible to talk without conveying what is really going on. It's also possible to say nothing at all, in which case it is even more difficult for partners to communicate.

One sure sign that things are not being talked about well is when conflicts seem to suddenly erupt over what appear to be insignificant matters. A backpacker named Eric told of a time he almost went berserk on a camping trip when the zipper on one of his backpack pockets became stuck and he couldn't get to his toothbrush. When his girlfriend Theresa tried first to help him with the zipper, then to cheer him up by joking about the problem, he turned on her angrily and blamed her for his reactions, and a long fight ensued. All for a recalcitrant pocket zipper and an inaccessible toothbrush?

Of course not. In fact, many factors contributed to this situation, but they were not apparent when the conflict itself burst forth because neither person had talked about feelings that preceded the conflict. In the weeks before the trip, Eric had been under a great deal of stress at work but he didn't tell Theresa because he didn't want work problems to interfere with their time together. In spite of that intention, he was nevertheless disturbed by thoughts of work and this tended to magnify his reaction to other things. Eric only recognized that the zipper wasn't really the issue when, after fifteen minutes of unproductive fighting, Theresa finally said, "This isn't like us to be fighting about something so silly. We better talk about what's really going on."

That statement—"we better talk about what's really going on"—is a key to both preventing and resolving conflicts in outdoor relationships. It opens the door to communication about things that have been held inside up to that point. With the door to communication opened, and with some awareness of how to improve the way we listen, we also need to consider how partners can talk in ways that strengthen and improve the relationship rather than increasing the conflicts we are hoping to prevent or resolve.

As with listening, most folks assume they already know how to talk to their partners, so they have nothing more to learn on the subject. Yet if one listens to verbal exchanges between partners, it is easy to recognize that there are large differences in how partners speak to each other. Whenever I met with outdoor partners who seemed to communicate especially well, I asked what worked well for them. Among the more valuable ideas that were offered are these:

RULES FOR TALKING SO PARTNERS CAN HEAR

- If something is on your mind, talk about it. Not speaking doesn't make the problem go away and your feelings will get out one way or another.
- Think before you speak and be mindful about both what you say and how you say it. Be careful about the tone of your voice and any sharp edges that might go with your words.
- Speak about your own thoughts and feelings, not about what the other person is doing "wrong." Phrase things in "I" terms, e.g., "I'm feeling" or "I would like to," not "you make me" or "it was you who."
- Ask, don't tell, your partners what they're feeling and how they think things can go better together.

- Look for the positives in the relationship. Be sure to talk about them and compliment your partners when things are going well or you appreciate something they do.

- If something isn't going well and needs to be talked about, it helps to start by recognizing what is going well and acknowledging that first.

- Reassure partners that you care about and value them and that is why you are talking about concerns. Then be sure your tone of voice and the things you say reflect that caring.

- Avoid the temptation for "gotcha's." You are not out to win or to prove who is right or wrong, you are trying to make things work better for both of you.

- Avoid the temptation to bring in "trigger" issues that you know will escalate the conflict rather than solve it.

- If you say or do something unkind or unfair, be willing to acknowledge and apologize. If your partner apologizes, be willing to forgive and move forward.

If partners would follow these guidelines when speaking to each other, many relationship accidents could be prevented or more easily resolved. However, once a conflict arises, it can be difficult to remember how we wanted to communicate with each other. What we need is a way to somehow get past the immediate issue that has provoked the conflict and find a way toward a resolution.

As a therapist, one of the most successful tools I have found for conflict resolution is to understand the difference between what people are saying and how they are communicating. Another way to describe this is by distinguishing between the content of the communication and the process of communication.

CONTENT AND PROCESS— THE "WHAT" AND "HOW" OF COMMUNICATION

The content of an interaction refers to the surface or literal meaning of the words that are exchanged. This is the "what" of communication and it tends to be the focus of most interactions. Communication that focuses primarily on content, particularly during conflicts, is unlikely to lead to understanding or resolution. The reason is that when people focus on content, they get "stuck" arguing about what was said or done and in the process pay almost no attention to the situational context, the ways things are said, or how each person is feeling.

By comparison, the process of an interaction refers to the ways things are said, the context of the interaction, how topics shift from one subject to another, and all of the non-verbal elements of communication. In general, we are more likely to find resolutions to problems when we attend to the process of the communication as well as to the content.

In the earlier example of Eric and Theresa, the stuck zipper was the surface content that initially appeared to upset Eric. But the processes that led up to that situation included all the stress he was under and the fact that he was not talking directly about any of those underlying issues. When Theresa observed that it wasn't like them to fight about something so silly, she was making a process observation. She was stepping away from the direct topic of the zipper in order to see the bigger context and pattern of the argument. This perspective allowed them to go beyond the immediate situation and content so they could get to what was really troubling them.

Another way to illustrate this idea is through the story of a couple who had been going camping and fishing together for almost twenty years. Although the two described their marriage as happy and said they really enjoyed fishing together, there was one situation that both agreed always led to difficulties: backing their boat trailer up to put in or take their fishing boat out of a lake or river.

As they described this event, Ed always drove the truck while his wife Helen walked alongside to give directions and keep the boat tethered. This apparently simple and often repeated task seemed to inevitably produce a fight. Either the trailer would jackknife, or the boat would drift, or something would not go just right and the two would wind up cursing the problem and yelling at each other.

> *"I told you to turn right," Helen would shout.*
> *"No, you didn't, you said left," Ed would respond.*
> *"No, you turned left, I saw you, but I said right."*
> *"Well, you were signaling left."*
> *"Is this left?" Helen replied, gesturing with her right hand.*

Arguments like this tend quickly to degenerate into the childish "did not"—"did so" format and are not likely to go anywhere positive. The next step is typically further explanation of why what one says is or was true while what the other says is false. At this point the goal has shifted from solving the problem to winning the argument. Now instead of working together to make things function better, partners are fighting against each other as each tries to win and make the other lose. Ultimately, genuine solutions are almost never achieved by such disputes. Instead, people simply tire of arguing and let the issue drop unresolved until the next time.

A much more productive approach is for partners to step back and look at the processes that led to the conflict and that are happening as part of the communication. Attending to what is happening in the activity can help prevent similar situations from being repeated in the future, while emphasis on the relationship can help identify any underlying problems that need to be addressed.

TALKING ABOUT THE ACTIVITY:
SOLVING PART OF THE PROBLEM

Imagine what would have happened for Ed and Helen if, instead of arguing about who said turn left or right, they had said, "You know, we always have an argument when we do this. What can we do differently to make this process work better next time?"

If they could get past blaming one another, they could look at the process of backing up the trailer and cooperatively review how they have been doing things all along and how the process could be improved. Maybe their system of signals or instructions lends itself to confusion and needs to be changed. Perhaps a better mirror or an improved trailer could make things easier. Whatever solution they discover, by looking at the process together and working jointly toward a solution, the problem is more likely to be solved and the relationship strengthened.

RELATIONSHIP PROCESSES:
TALKING ABOUT WHAT REALLY MATTERS

Focusing on processes within an activity can help make that activity go better, but there may still be underlying relationship issues that need to be addressed. In the case of Ed and Helen, why was it that instead of finding a better way to back up the boat, their arguments for twenty years had focused on who was right and who was wrong? What does it say about relationships if people are using a harsh tone of voice or are saying things designed to hurt each other's feelings?

Whether or not we find a solution to make a specific activity work better, what really matters in the long run is finding ways to make relationships go well. Keeping in mind the distinction between process and content can help us work toward finding relationship solutions. For example, if a conflict has developed, partners could go beyond the immediate situation and start to work on relationship issues by saying something like, "Hey, we're arguing about something that's not really that important and we're not treating each other very well. I think we need to talk about that." Or, "I know you're frustrated about getting to the trail late, but it hurts my feelings when you treat me the way you have been." Or, "I feel like you make all the decisions without involving me and that's frustrating." Statements such as these shift the focus from the surface issue to the relationship process. From there, partners can begin to talk about what's going on between them as people rather than what's going on in the activity.

GIVE THINGS TIME WHILE STAYING TOGETHER

Applying the suggestions for improving how we listen and talk with partners can go a long way toward resolving relationship accidents, but sometimes emotions are so charged that effective, caring communication is almost impossible. Under those circumstances, the best advice may be to give each person time and space to cool down and reflect on what has happened.

One couple told me that they had established an inviolable "time-out" rule. If, in the middle of a discussion, one or both feel things are getting out of hand or they need some space to think, they can call a time-out and the interaction is temporarily halted. By mutual agreement, time-outs can only be used if the purpose is to help rather than hinder communication. Also, they can never be used as weapons and they cannot be indefinite. At some point, the partners have to resume talking.

Whether "time-outs" are initiated by mutual agreement or because people become so upset they quit speaking together, partners must find a way to stay together no matter how angry they may be with one another. In our homes, we can go to another room or take a walk to get some space, but in the outdoors people can die when parties become separated. Not long ago, a fatality occurred when communication broke down among a group of climbers and one went off on his own. Shortly thereafter, the weather closed, visibility was lost, and the rest of the party were unable to make contact with the one who had left. Several days of extensive searches failed to find the climber and it was assumed he must have perished in a fall or died of exposure.

If communications break down so thoroughly that there seems no way to resolve the situation at the moment, one or both partners should acknowledge that fact, swallow their anger or pride, and say something like: "I'm sorry. I'm not doing a very good job of working things out right now and I know we're both very upset. What do we need to do to call a truce for now so we can work together?"

It may not be easy to apologize, take the blame, or let go of hurt feelings, but partners must do whatever it takes to stay together and deal with the realities of the outdoors together even though for the moment they may not feel like occupying the same planet. Later, when the situation is safer, the conflict can be revisited and perhaps resolved more easily. After spending time working together without arguing, most partners find they are more able to see both sides of the situation and are willing to talk constructively about how to move forward.

UNDERSTANDING THE COMMUNICATION MODELS WE LEARNED FROM

In spite of our best efforts to communicate well, we may still find ourselves speaking or acting in ways we or our partners are not happy with. When this occurs, it can be extremely helpful to reflect on how we learned to communicate and how our own outdoor relationships may be shaped by the models our parents provided. As one woman said about how she communicates with her partner, "It feels like my mother hides in my backpack and jumps out to say things I really didn't mean to say." Her partner offered a similar observation, "Even as I say something, I can almost hear my father's voice coming out. It's eerie."

One way to understand where our models for relationships and communication come from is for partners to talk with each other about how their parents communicated, what kinds of situations were associated with conflicts or good times, and how those early models may relate to present interactions. Sometimes natural conditions provide a perfect opportunity for this discussion.

One couple, Tim and Susan, told how they learned about each other's families while spending a long night together in a snow cave. With nothing better to do, and an eternity of winter darkness to wait out, they started sharing early memories of family camping trips. As they talked, they began to realize that some of the issues that caused problems in their relationship were very similar to those they remembered from childhood. Tim recalled how his father always had a critical edge to his voice and seemed to treat his mother like she was never quite competent enough. When he said this, his partner Susan somewhat hesitantly shared that she felt like Tim treated her that way sometimes. Susan went on to say that this was especially hard for her because she had been raised by a hypercritical, emotionally abusive father. As a result, she was sensitive to any criticism and was afraid to stand up for herself. She also shared that she had initially been reluctant to go camping with Tim because her memories of camping with her family were very unpleasant.

For this couple, discussion of parental models happened almost by coincidence. For partners wishing to explore this issue more purposefully, it may be useful to consider questions such as the following.

FAMILY MODELS REVIEW

- What are your favorite memories of the outdoors with parents or other family members?
- What unpleasant memories do you have of the outdoors with parents or others?
- What personal characteristics of your parents did you admire or hope to find in yourself or your partner?
- What characteristics did your parents lack that you hoped to find in a partner?
- Finally, describe any personal characteristics that you disliked about your parents and hoped you would not find in your partner.

Reviewing questions like these together may bring up sensitive material, but it is important for partners to be aware of how each person's background influences current relationships and communications. With this awareness, we can begin to alter patterns that may have been creating problems for many years.

COMMUNICATION IN FAMILIES

When we realize how our relationships and communications are affected by the models our parents provided, we are more likely to also recognize the importance of providing good models for our own families. If parents yell at each other, don't listen to one another, argue to win rather than solve problems, or put each other down, they should not be surprised if children treat each other or even their parents in the same way. By the same token, if parents set a positive example of how to talk and listen and solve problems together, children are more likely to follow that example. Suggestions offered in this chapter can go a long way toward improving communications of all family members, but parents need to give specific attention to children's emotional needs, cognitive abilities, and positions within the family hierarchy.

LISTENING TO CHILDREN

Skilled parents know the importance of listening so children feel heard. One of the ways they do this is by repeating back what the child says. For example, if a young child excitedly tells a story about finding a frog in a stream, a receptive parent might open her eyes almost as wide as the child's, share the enthusiasm, and say, "You found a frog in a stream? Wow, that's neat."

With older children, listening is just as important, but in addition to reflecting what the child says, parents can show interest by asking questions or in some other way encouraging the youngster to expand. If questions are asked, they shouldn't make the child feel put on the spot or grilled for information. The purpose is to show the parent's interest and validate the child's excitement or wonder.

Perhaps even more important than what the parent says in response to a child is what the parent is doing while listening. Too often when children begin to tell us something, we are thinking of or doing other things. Sometimes this is unavoidable, but it is worth asking ourselves how often we give our children only half our attention instead of listening fully. It is also worth asking if what we are doing instead of listening is really more urgent than giving a child a feeling they are important and heard as people.

In a campground at Yellowstone National Park, I observed two simultaneous but very different examples of listening when a group of excited children came running through the camp shouting to their parents that they had just seen a bear. One parent immediately stopped what he was doing, turned to the children, and took in all the excitement they had to share. He asked where they had seen it, what color it was, and how big, and responded with animated facial and body expressions. Then, even though he had been in the middle of setting up their camp, and even though I knew from an earlier conversation that he had seen bears many times himself, he said excitedly, "Let's go back and see if he's still there." With that, they were off together.

By comparison, half of the original group of kids had gone to an adjacent trailer and told their father the same exciting news, but were met with, "I'm not surprised. The park's famous for 'em. Now, give me a hand setting things up. Hand me that tool so I can get the trailer level." The children dutifully followed the instruction but even though they tried to keep telling the story, one could feel the abrupt change in energy. If the children in the first group grow up to love nature, while those in the second have a different reaction, it would not be hard to understand why.

While time and attention can go a long way toward encouraging communication with children, it is sometimes necessary for parents to also help kids give voice to what they are feeling. For this to be effective, parents must be able to put themselves in the child's position and try to understand what the child might be feeling.

Suppose, for example, that a family is on a camping trip and one of the children seems to be quite moody. A parent might sense this, become upset with the child, and insist that the child "snap out of it." Or the parent might notice the child's state, then quietly give some thought to what has been happening or what the child has been experiencing. Then the parent might gently observe, "What's the matter, Chris, you seem to be out of sorts? You want to talk about anything?"

If the child doesn't identify a problem, the parent may help by sharing his or her observations of what's been happening: "Hmm. I notice that you and the other kids aren't playing much together today. Are you feeling kind of left out?"

It isn't necessary for the parent to be exactly right in guessing what might be going on. What matters most is that the parent shows an interest in how things are going and is prepared to listen to the child. That communication of caring is what the child needs more than anything else, and as long as it is there, most situations can be managed well.

TALKING WITH CHILDREN

The other side of listening to children is how we speak to them. There is no "best" way to talk to children, but there are some general principles that can make communications work better. The first principle is, again, to model the kinds of behaviors you expect from your children. If you want children to treat you, their siblings, and others courteously, communicating courteously with the children is a good place to start. This is a simple concept, but one that is often overlooked.

Saying "please" when making a request of the child, using a gentle tone of voice, and other such signs of respect and consideration make a large difference in the quality and effects of what we say.

All people are thinking, feeling beings who want to be respected. If we make a reasonable request or statement to someone who then responds with a short answer and no explanation, we're likely to become upset. The same is true of children. When plans are made, children are much more likely to go along with them if the reasons are explained and the explanation shows that the children's needs and interests are considered. This does not mean that decisions will always go the children's way, but it does mean that their concerns are acknowledged and taken into account and this is communicated to them.

I watched these principles in action as two parents interacted with their three children on a backpacking trip to a high mountain lake. The family had apparently planned to spend two nights at the lake, but by the afternoon of the second day, the children were growing restless and complaining that they wanted to go home. Their parents listened attentively to the children's concerns, then said, "We understand you're feeling bored right now, so you want to go home tonight. There are a couple of things to consider, though. First, the two of us are having a good time here and would really like to stay for even more days if we could. Second, it's late in the afternoon and we probably would just barely make it to the car by dark. Then we'd have a long drive home and wouldn't get there till very late tonight. For those reasons, we think it's best to stay here tonight like we planned originally, so that's what we're going to do. We'll head out tomorrow around noon. If you like, for this afternoon in a little while we can play some games or go for a hike, or maybe you kids can find something to do together."

These parents showed they understood their children's concerns and were willing to share their thinking with the children. Of course, this does not mean the children suddenly agreed with their parents' plans. In fact, and not surprisingly, the parents' explanation and decision were met by grumbling and whining and attempts to change the decision. To expect otherwise would have been unrealistic, so the parents did not feel a need to tell their children to not complain. Instead, they simply repeated that they would be at their camp till the next day and left it at that.

The parents knew it was possible to listen to children and respect their interests, yet still be direct and decisive. They also knew that when the children realized the decision had been made, they would probably find some way to make the most of it. Within fifteen minutes of having cried about being bored and wanting to go, one of the kids had invented a game of throwing pine cones at a target made of sticks. That kept them busy until they all went hiking, and the rest of the day passed happily. The next day, when it was time to leave, all the children protested that they wanted to stay. They even used their parents' former statement of that same desire in their negotiations, but the demands of work were waiting and they had to leave. The parents also knew that even if they had not had to work the next day, it is always good to leave children wanting more so they will be eager to go the next time.

CONTENT AND PROCESS IN COMMUNICATIONS WITH CHILDREN

Another communication principle that is equally important in families is the distinction between process and content, the "what" and "how" of communication. Awareness of this distinction can be a lifesaver for parents who find themselves repeatedly boxed in by children who seem to be natural junior debaters. If a parent says something or makes a decision and finds that a child starts to engage in a lengthy debate or negotiation, process awareness helps the parent step out of the content of the negotiation and recognize what is happening. For example, a parent might say, "Wait a second, please, I asked you if you could help me set up the tent, and you answered by asking why your sister didn't have to. Your sister is not the issue. The real issue is that I need help here and I expect you to pitch in. If you want to talk about how work is shared, we can do that, but only after we get this done."

With greater process awareness, parents can also begin to include process statements in their communications and thereby influence not only what will be communicated but how. This can be particularly helpful if a parent is feeling tired or worn out and might have a short fuse. I saw a parent use this successfully at a lunch counter in a ski lodge by saying, "Okay, we've already talked about how much we have to spend for lunch, and to be honest I'm pretty tired already. So each of you get what you want within your limit and please let's not be asking for any more."

Process statements that structure communication are also very important in emergency situations with children. For example, in an emergency, a parent might begin a statement to children with, "This is very important, so I want everyone to listen carefully and then do what I tell you. We don't have time to argue, so I need you to just do this and then I'll explain things later." Obviously, this sort of statement should be reserved for special situations lest it be overused and lose its usefulness in real emergencies.

BALANCING INVOLVEMENT WITH AUTHORITY

Opinions differ about how to strike a balance between a completely authoritarian family in which parents set all the rules and children have no say versus a completely democratic structure in which children's wishes carry equal weight to that of parents. In general, research and most experts on the subject suggest that a point somewhere in the middle of these extremes yields the best results. Parents have more knowledge and experience in life and they are responsible for their families. It follows, therefore, that they need to make certain decisions about what is best for the children and the family. On the other hand, children are people too and they have their own needs and ideas that should be taken into account and respected.

There are many things in the outdoors in which parents can give children a say. Deciding what kinds of trail foods to bring, where to go, the colors of gear, etc., can easily involve input from children. But there are also things children may not be able to decide. For example, if it's raining and a child who gets wet now might later become chilled, parents may have to insist the child wear rain gear. Or, if a child wants to race ahead but the trail is dangerous or the child might become lost, the parents may require the child to stay close.

Successful parents are those who know how to give children a voice and respect their interests but are also willing to make choices and set ground rules that provide a structure and secure base. As children become older and more experienced in the outdoors, parents can give them more responsibility, but this should be a gradual process that builds upon the smaller decisions structured earlier in their lives.

PARENTS ARE HUMANS

It's always easier to write about communicating with children than it is to actually do so. Even the most conscientious and skilled parents can have bad days or can simply miss something important about their children. When this happens, parents can still provide important modeling by being willing to apologize.

One parent told how he had been so busy with an important project for his work that he gave his daughter only half-hearted attention when she told him about an upcoming camping trip her scout troop was planning. Thinking about their interaction later that evening, he took time out to approach his daughter again and ask about her plans. He also apologized for not having given her his attention earlier. The daughter was at first reluctant to talk any more about the matter, but with some gentle questioning she began to tell more about the trip. By the end of the conversation, she was again showing the enthusiasm that she'd had earlier. As the father tucked her in that night, she thanked him for talking with her and said she understood that he was busy earlier.

The best we can do as parents is do our best. We're bound to make mistakes, but if we communicate concern, are willing to listen, and can acknowledge errors as we go, things usually work out pretty well.

COMMUNICATION IN GROUPS

One of my hopes is that one day good communication principles will become part of the essential skills for all those who participate in outdoor activities. Just as we would train physically and learn to use ropes and other equipment before climbing, we would give equal attention to learning how to listen and speak with our partners.

Unfortunately, we're still far from that stage. It is rare for outdoor groups, whether they're informal groups of friends or well-established organizations, to purposefully and explicitly talk about how members communicate with one another. This means that one of the first things that can be done to improve communication in groups is to begin talking about talking.

TEACHING AND TALKING ABOUT COMMUNICATION FROM THE START

There are lots of ways to get group members talking about communication with each other. When I'm with a group of friends or leading a group of students on an outing, before we get under way I initiate a brief conversation by saying something like, "One thing that's very important is that we all work together as well as we can and help each other. If anyone has any concerns, questions, or anything else on your mind, I hope you'll tell someone about it. And if we need to make decisions or change plans along the way, my preference is to talk about that together so everyone knows what we're doing and feels part of it."

After introducing the topic, I ask if anyone has something to discuss at that moment. I might also ask if anyone feels there is a reason he or she would not feel comfortable talking about concerns along the way. Lest someone be reluctant to raise such concerns, I emphasize that we need to do this before we start the outing because everyone's safety and enjoyment depend on our communication together. If something does come up that suggests people might not be open to talking with one another, we talk about why and what could be done to change things.

Another way to promote discussion of communication in groups is to include it as part of other training activities. When I work with groups as a leader or instructor, I make it a point to teach listening, speaking, and other communication skills along with the other technical skills or equipment information. As a leader it is also particularly important to model good communication skills. If leaders or instructors don't demonstrate positive communication skills, students or other group members are less likely to do so.

GROUP COMMUNICATION DURING ACTIVITIES

Once an outing is underway, group members need to monitor interactions and be aware of communication processes that are not constructive. If you're in a group in which people aren't communicating or getting along, you might find an opportunity to talk on the side with those involved and see what is going on. Sometimes an informal "mediator" can help people work through an impasse or see things in a different way.

As group members it's also helpful to be open to feedback from our partners. Just as we should accept suggestions when we're learning new outdoor skills, we should also be amenable to suggestions about our communication skills. It might not be easy to have a friend say, "Hey, Brian, what's up? You've really been short with people today," but it is much better for the friend to recognize something is wrong and try to help than for me to be stuck in some pattern without realizing it.

One group with whom I spoke was well ahead of the curve on this and actually appointed a "crab monitor" on every trip. This person's job was to keep tabs on how everyone was getting along and to award "crab points" if someone was being particularly cranky. At the end of the trip the person with the most points had to buy everyone drinks. That same person then had to serve as monitor on the next trip.

This approach served two important functions and allowed people to laugh in the middle of what might otherwise have been tense moments. The first function was to make people aware that the quality of interactions was important and everyone needed to try to talk respectfully with one another, work together, and get along. The second function was to provide an outside perspective. It's much easier to be rude if we know everyone else will be too embarrassed to say or do anything. But if we know that rudeness or negative communications will be recognized and called to our attention, we're more likely to monitor ourselves and use the kinds of principles described in this chapter.

The other side to monitoring for negative communications is watching for positive communications and letting people know they're appreciated. If people communicate well with one another, it never hurts to acknowledge this. Saying something as simple as "I really liked the way you said that" or "thanks for listening" lets partners know we're aware of how they're communicating and their efforts are valued.

NEW ROUTES REVISITED

In the introduction, I suggested that we need to consider new standards for what excellence means in outdoor relationships. Perhaps the process of communication can provide such a standard. Imagine what it would mean if, rather than evaluating our performance against the difficulty of a climb, the rating of a river, or the steepness of a ski run, we chose instead to set the quality of our relationships as the most important goal and recognized communication as the technique through which we reach that goal.

This would mean a radical change from how we have traditionally approached outdoor activities. Of course, we could still continue to pursue all of the other reasons that draw us to the outdoors, but we would do so from a different perspective. Instead of focusing primarily on the destination, we would attend more to the journey. In place of external standards of difficulty, we would look inward at the quality of our relationships.

This idea might sound strange to some, but in fact it has always been a part of the outdoors. When we read about great adventures, what draws us in is not the technical details. Instead, we are drawn by the story of people struggling together to meet difficult challenges. Ultimately, the story of outdoor adventure comes down to a story of humans and how we define ourselves. For a very few individuals, the definition of who they are comes from extraordinary achievements. But even those who climb the highest must eventually come down. Then, like the rest of us, what matters most will be the stories that are lived every day in relationships.

APPENDIX: GETTING HELP

*"It wasn't just when we were outdoors. It was all the time.
No matter what we did, we couldn't get along.
That's when we decided to see a therapist."*

*"I didn't really think we'd get much out of it. But I can honestly tell
you it's the best thing we ever did. It was hard. Really hard.
But I don't think we'd be together if we hadn't gotten some help,
and I really believe things are much better now than they were."*

MY HOPE IS THAT PEOPLE WHO READ THIS BOOK and put into place the suggestions will be more able to enjoy their relationships and their outdoor activities together. At the same time, however, books can only go so far and there will be times when additional assistance is needed. One way to find such assistance is by seeing a therapist. For those who might be considering therapy, this appendix discusses when therapists should be seen, why people may be reluctant to pursue therapy, how to select a therapist, and how to make the most out of the therapy experience.

KNOWING WHEN WE NEED MORE HELP

Outdoor activities can pose unique challenges for relationships, but what happens in the outdoors is ultimately connected to what is going on in relationships as a whole. What is more, the way we deal with problems in outdoor relationships can tell us a lot about whether we could benefit from some form of professional assistance.

A question I sometimes use to help people consider whether to see a therapist is: "If you were to identify the most important ways you would like to change yourself or your relationships, what would those be?" Then I ask, "What has prevented the changes you want from happening in the past and what can help make things different in the future?"

These questions can be answered in many different ways, but it's important to be honest with ourselves. Many people are able to identify changes they would like to make, but when it comes to how they will bring those changes about, the answers are rather vague or uncertain. If we knew how to bring about the changes we want, we would probably have done so already. The fact that we haven't suggests that something may be blocking our efforts or that we may not really know exactly what we want or how to get there. If that is the case, therapy may be in order.

WHY PEOPLE DON'T SEE THERAPISTS

Some people are very open to the idea of therapy, but many are quite resistant. Those who haven't been to therapy before don't know what it involves or what might happen. Even though our lives as individuals or our relationships might have problems, the problems are at least familiar. Therapy, by its nature, suggests that changes can and should be made, but we cannot know beforehand if we will like those changes.

Of course, there are no guarantees, but hundreds of research studies show that most people who have been through therapy believe it was a worthwhile and positive experience. As a man who reluctantly entered therapy later acknowledged: "I was dead sure it wouldn't work, and I was almost ready to call it quits rather than see a 'shrink.' But I'm glad I didn't. I actually learned some things that I didn't even know there was to learn and we really are happier now—happier than we've ever been, in fact."

Along with fears of the unknown, many partners are concerned about therapy because they believe the therapist is likely to "take sides" and blame one person for all the problems. In some relationships, it is true that one person's behaviors are more problematic and must be changed for the relationship to work. This is the case in abusive relationships or when one member of a couple has a significant personality disorder. In most therapy, however, the problem is not solely one person's. Rather, it involves how partners interact and communicate with one another.

When I speak with people who are reluctant to participate in therapy because they're afraid they will be criticized by their partner, I sometimes ask if there aren't some things they would also like to talk with their partner about but have not felt able to. This helps people realize that therapy should be a two-way street. Each person has the opportunity to talk about her or his feelings and needs and the therapist is present, not to pass judgments, but to help the interaction stay constructive.

The key is to recognize that therapy is an opportunity to address and better understand issues that may have long posed problems for the relationship and may well have existed prior to the relationship. Because we are human, all of us have at least some such issues, and not dealing with them will not make them go away.

FINDING AND CHOOSING A THERAPIST

If individuals or partners accept that therapy might be beneficial, the next task is finding the "right" therapist. This is not always easy. When someone says, "You should see a therapist," what they really mean is you should see a "good" therapist.

Among the professions that may be qualified to work with relationship issues are clinical psychologists, marriage and family therapists, social workers, counselors, and pastoral counselors with degrees from accredited programs. Be aware that in some states virtually anyone who wants to can call him or herself a therapist or counselor and charge for services even though he or she may have had very little or no training. Therefore, it is always advisable to take the steps listed below to verify qualifications before selecting someone to work with.

QUALIFICATIONS CHECKLIST

1. Many insurance policies include coverage for certain types of therapists. Before selecting a therapist, check with your insurer to see if coverage is included in your policy and if the insurer has a list of recommended or approved providers.
2. If you find someone you are thinking of seeing, check to be sure he or she has at least a masters degree. The reason for this is that in most cases those who hold bachelor's degrees have received only minimal training and often no supervision in actual clinical work.
3. Check with the state licensing agency to ensure the person is

licensed to practice under the title she or he claims. While you check on this, ask the licensing agency to briefly tell you just what is required to obtain that license in that state.

4. Check to be sure that the person obtained his or her degree from a program that is formally accredited by the pertinent national professional organization. This helps reduce the chance that someone who claims to have a doctorate or masters degree received his or her diploma from a "mail-order" university.

5. Check with the state professional association to see if the individual is a member and is included in their referral listing. Not all professionals are members of their association, and it is not required that they be so in order to practice, but membership in such organizations is a sign the person is committed and involved in the profession.

6. Finally, ask the individual directly what specific training or experience he or she has had in working with couples, families, or the specific issues for which you are seeking therapy.

This may sound like a lot of work, but it is worth the effort to be sure you are receiving therapy from a qualified person. In most instances, these questions can be answered relatively quickly with just a few phone calls. You needn't be embarrassed about asking these questions because it is a professional's responsibility to provide clients with this information. If someone seems hesitant or resistant to telling you his or her own qualifications, perhaps you should seek assistance somewhere else.

MAKING THE MOST OF THERAPY

When you see a therapist, you'll want to make the most of the experience. The best way to do this is to remember that therapy can be challenging, sometimes painful work and you are not there for the therapist to "fix" you or your partner, "solve" your problems, or play "judge" or "referee." You are in therapy for the therapist to help you understand yourself, your partner, and your relationship, and for you and your partner to discover ways together to make things work better.

For therapy to be effective, partners need to be willing to risk talking about issues that they may be reluctant or embarrassed to discuss. If you go to therapy but keep the things that concern you most inside, it will be difficult for you or your partner to make any progress in those areas.

Along with being willing to talk openly about your thoughts, feelings, or concerns, it also helps to keep in mind that you are free to tell the therapist what you think would help you most. Different therapists follow different theoretical models and not every approach works well for every individual, couple, or family. If you're seeing someone who you feel gives too much advice, you can say so. Or if you feel a therapist does not offer enough input, you could say that as well. Similarly, if someone feels that a therapist does not understand his or her position or is "taking the other person's side," the solution isn't to stop going entirely. Rather, it is to raise that concern in therapy and work it through together with the therapist and with your partner.

Because therapy raises issues that have long been kept under the surface, sessions can often be emotionally draining and there may be times you won't want to continue. That is perfectly understandable, but it is very important to stay with the process and not give up if things get hard. Research clearly shows that people who stay in therapy are more likely to benefit than those who drop out prematurely. In this same context, watch out as well for what therapists call "flight into health." This term refers to the tendency of clients in therapy to suddenly experience a "miracle cure" and claim that all of their problems have been solved in the first couple sessions so they do not need to keep coming. Often, what has actually happened in such cases is that therapy was starting to address the real issues and this became frightening. Rather than face those issues, one or both partners made a sudden change in surface behavior that produced a temporary improvement. The problem is that this sudden change is unlikely to last. When the luster of the miracle cure fades, as it inevitably will, the same old problems will be back.

THE GOALS OF THERAPY

As you approach therapy, keep in mind that real and lasting change can take time. The old days of analysis five times a week for years and years are largely behind us now, but to expect a "cure" in one or two sessions is probably not realistic either. On average, most people who stay with therapy and make significant progress will see a therapist for somewhere between five to fifteen or twenty sessions spread out over several months or longer, depending on their needs. Many people also come back to their therapist from time to time as new experiences bring up issues that had not been addressed before or that seemed to have been resolved but emerged again. This is nothing to be embarrassed or ashamed about. Rather, it is part of the normal process of change.

The goal of therapy can be defined as: "Helping people understand and experience who they are, who they have been, and who they would like to become." In a very real sense, therapy has been successful when you no longer need the therapist—when you've developed the skills and insights to better understand yourself and your partner, and when you can use that understanding to make constructive changes. Ultimately, therapy is part of the longer journey of our lives. The challenge and opportunity before each of us is to make the most of that journey.

INDEX

ABOUT THE AUTHOR

A licensed clinical psychologist with more than fifteen years of experience, Brian Baird is Chair of the Department of Psychology at Pacific Lutheran University in Tacoma, Washington. An avid participant in many outdoor activities, including skiing, backpacking, climbing, kayaking, and bicycling, he has been a ski instructor as well as a group leader for sea kayaking expeditions.

OTHER TITLES YOU MAY ENJOY
FROM THE MOUNTAINEERS

Kids in the Wild: A Family Guide to Outdoor Recreation, Ross & Gladfelter.
A comprehensive, kid-tested parents' guide to sharing outdoor adventures with children of all ages and skill levels.

Mountain Trivia Challenge, Storer.
Go head-to-head with friends and family on facts about mountain weather, famous and lesser-known mountaineers, mountains in the movies, and more!

***Outdoor Family Guide*™** series.
Popular adventure guides for families and groups, including information on hikes, nature trails, and year-round activities such as rafting, camping, horseback riding, skiing, and cycling. Includes:
The Southwest's Four Corners, Wharton.
Lake Tahoe, Evans.

***100 Hikes*™** series
Best-selling mountain hiking guides, with fully detailed trail descriptions, directions, maps, and photos. Includes:
The Alps, Spring & Edwards.
Arizona, Warren.
California's Central Sierra and Coast Range, Spring.
Colorado, Warren.
Inland Northwest, Landers & Dolphin.
Northern California, Soares & Soares.
Oregon, Ostertag.
Washington's Alpine Lakes, Spring, Manning & Spring.
Washington's North Cascades: Glacier Peak Region, Spring & Manning.
Washington's North Cascades National Park Region, Spring & Manning.
Washington's South Cascades and Olympics, Spring & Manning.

Best Hikes With Children™ series

100 easily-accessible hikes, many lesser-known, with detailed trail information. Tips on hiking with kids, safety, and wilderness ethics. Includes:

Catskills and Hudson River Valley, Lewis.
Colorado, Keilty.
Connecticut, Massachusetts & Rhode Island, Lewis.
New Jersey, Zatz.
New Mexico, Julyan.
Sacramento, McMillon.
San Francisco's North Bay, McMillon.
San Francisco's South Bay, McMillon.
Utah, Keilty.
Vermont, New Hampshire & Maine, Lewis.
Western and Central Oregon, Henderson.
Western Washington and the Cascades, Vol., I & II, Burton.

The **Mountaineers Books** is the largest publisher of outdoor books in the country, with more than 300 titles in print. Titles range from outdoor instruction and safety manuals to guides for hiking and bicycling through international destinations. The Mountaineers Books also publishes volumes on mountaineering history, natural history, and environmental and conservation issues. For more information, contact The Mountaineers Books at 1001 SW Klickitat Way, Seattle, WA 98134. Phone (206) 223-6303. Fax (206) 223-6306.